The Indispensability of Virtue

Donald DeMarco

En Route Books and Media, LLC
Saint Louis, MO

✺ENROUTE
Make the time

En Route Books and Media, LLC
5705 Rhodes Avenue
St. Louis, MO 63109

Contact us at
contactus@enroutebooksandmedia.com

Cover Credit: Sebastian Mahfood using "Praying Hands" (1508), Albrecht Dürer (1471-1528)

Copyright 2025 Donald DeMarco

ISBN-13: 979-8-88870-454-7
Library of Congress Control Number:
Available online at http://catalog.loc.gov

All rights reserved. No part of this book may be reproduced, stored in a retrieval system, or transmitted in any form, or by any means, electronic, mechanical, photocopying, or otherwise, without the prior written permission of the author.

Dedication

This book is dedicated to Mary, my faithful wife of 58 years, mother of 5, and grandmother of 14.

Acknowledgement

The author wishes to thank Angie, Tom, Joe, Paul, Gerald, Deidre, Maurits, Joseph, and Sebastian for their assistance and encouragement.

Epigraphs

"All the gold which is under or upon the earth is not enough to give in exchange for virtue."

Plato

"No people can be great who have ceased to be virtuous."

Samuel Johnson

"Sweet are the slumbers of the virtuous man."

Joseph Addison

"The superior man thinks always of virtue; the common man thinks of comfort."

Confucius

Table of Contents

Introduction 1

Prayer: Should God Have an E-mail Address? 3

Justice: The Disadvantages of Being Invisible 7

Mercy: Charting the Mercy of God 11

Fidelity: Can There Be a Replacement for Religion? 15

Hope: Clarifying Two Meanings of Hope 19

Resourcefulness: On Overcoming Laziness 23

Authenticity: The Dethronement of Man 27

Belief: Clarifying Two Kinds of Belief 31

Neighborliness: The Central Problem in Life 35

Faith: What Is the Moon Saying? 39

Reverence: What are the Stars Saying? 43

Love: What neither Plato nor Aristotle Realized 47

Morality: The Role of Morality, According to Jacques Maritain, in Forming a True Democracy 51

Wisdom: A Mother's Wisdom: The Amazing Story of Thomas Edison 57

Teaching: Is Teaching the Same Thing as Imposing? 61

Humanism: Has Secular Humanism Overtaken Christian Humanism? 65

Heroism: Baseball's Good Samaritan 69

Courage: How Fear Leads to Failure 73

Brotherhood: Am I My Brother's Keeper? 77

Studiousness: What Books Should I Read? 81

Sociability: Economics and Politics, the Vital Difference 85

Kindness: Acts of Kindness Can Save Our Souls 89

Spirituality: Silence and Spirituality 93

Artistry: Banishing the Bard 97

Strength: Superman in Perspective 101

Holiness: The Meaning of Holiness 105

Honesty: Knowledge and Wisdom 109

Mortality: The Stars Also Perish 113

Confidence: Doorway to a Doubtful Future? 117

Education: Compulsory Miseducation 121

Freedom: The Freedom to Say No 125

Fairness: Abortion and the Golden Rule 129

Introduction

Virtue, in a word, is strength. For Shakespeare, "Virtue is bold." Virtue gives us the ability to do the right thing at the right time. A person's character consists of the various virtues he has cultivated.

Virtue is variable and versatile. There is a virtue for every moral challenge. We need courage in the face of danger, wisdom in a crisis, love for all occasions, and kindness on a daily basis.

This book is a series of 32 highly distinctive articles. Each one of them centers on a virtue or a virtuous activity. Its aim is to make virtue attractive as well as dramatic, by demonstrating its importance in a variety of situations. We should all aspire to be virtuous, for it is through virtues that we become fully ourselves. Indeed, virtue is indispensable.

Dr. Donald DeMarco
February 22, 2025

Prayer

Should God Have an E-mail Address?

Many have implored the Church to be up-to-date. Would it be impertinent to ask God to be up-to-date? If He had an e-mail address, people could ask Him questions and expect a quick, but satisfactory response. God allowed the e-mail system to be created. Would it not be reasonable, as well as most helpful to people, if He made use of this splendid development? It would be indeed gratifying to people, as well as exciting, to go to their computer or iPad and receive an e-mail from heaven. Would this not be a huge boon to religion in general?

It is easy to fantasize reasons for God having an e-mail address. The fact that He does not indicates that he should not. And there must be a good reason for not having this innovative system of electronic communication.

St. Thomas Aquinas takes up the question whether Christ should have committed his doctrine to writing. An e-mail response, naturally, would require writing. Hence, Aquinas would have been opposed to God writing e-mail messages. He offers his reasons in his *Summa Theologica*, III, Q. 42, a.4. Because of being the most excellent of teachers, it was fitting that He imprint "His doctrine in the hearts of the hearers." He also states that if Christ had committed his doctrine to writing, "Men would have no deeper thought of His doctrine than that which appears on the surface of the writing. Aquinas offers a third reason. It was appropriate that His teaching would be passed on in an orderly manner: "Himself teaching His disciples immediately, and they subsequently teaching others by preaching and writing."

The question concerning God having his own e-mail address has been taken up by a number of people. In most cases, it seems, their answers are in the negative. One dissenter reasons that, "He isn't going to repeat the Bible by e-mail. That would be redundant. Everything he wants to say to us can be found in the Bible." Another surmises that e-mail would be repetitive, stating that "The Bible is the best way to get a message from God, and all it takes is going to your local library or church and is totally free online." Yet another remarks that a divine e-mail address would be confusing to an atheist: "Dear God. I just want to let you know that I'm sorry for not believing you because science said otherwise. But since you've set up and email account, I guess there's no choice but to believe that you exist." Finally, a person with common sense and a touch of humor maintains that, "God doesn't answer email; he only answers knee-mail. I saw that on a church sign once; it made me laugh pretty good."

God has provided us with the Gospel. This gift alone renders a divine e-mail system unnecessary. The Bible has been translated into every known language. This is what is available to everyone, not iPads or computers.

The comment concerning "knee-mail" brings to the discussion the notion of prayer. Prayer is communion with God. It obviates the need for e-mail. We distinguish communion from contact, communication, and community. Contact is the most superficial relationship we have with others. It is akin to "getting in touch." We contact our lawyer or a potential donor through the telephone. We may proceed to communicate with them, which is simply the passage of information from one person to another. Communication, however, is without communion. I may communicate something to another so that he knows what I am saying, but he does not know *me*. A community is a group of people living together with a common purpose. Nonetheless, it does not attain the level of communion since what defines community is merely togetherness. Communion is a special union in which both parties know each other as persons. If God had an e-mail address, there would be communication without communion. God prefers communion. The "Communion of Saints" is far more than a mere community.

During the Mass, a priest may communicate a rousing sermon, but the center and highpoint of the Mass is Holy Communion, an intimate and prayerful form of being united with Christ. The utilization of orbiting satellites to expand worldwide communication is a remarkable technological achievement. But it functions on the level of communication. The Eucharist is incomparably more remarkable since it brings into communion the finite and the Infinite, the temporal, and the Eternal, earth and Heaven, man and God.

Loneliness is pandemic. There are hotlines available for those who suffer from anomie. One may contact such a hotline and proceed to communicate with an adviser. But what is fundamentally needed is communion with another. Such communion is nothing other than love. Communication implies separation. Communion implies union. The biblical notion that "It is not good for man to be alone" well applies to communication without communion. The pain of loneliness is not adequately assuaged through images, messages, or engaging distractions. It cries out for what the philosopher

Gabriel Marcel refers to as "co-presence." Being present to each other is a form of communion that far transcends sharing e-mail messages.

Saint John Paul II referred to the central problem of modern life as a tension between "alienation" and "participation." Despite the elaborate modes of communication in our wired world, even the "high-fidelity" kind, alienation persists. Participation, for John Paul, means the participation in the humanity of another person.

Whether God should have an e-mail address may sound like a silly question. But its negative answer is not so silly.

Justice

The Disadvantages of Being Invisible

The prospect of being invisible is tantalizing to most people. It would mean the separation of punishment from crime. One could steal with impunity and build up a large fortune. But this is just one way in which the invisible man could violate the moral law and remain unpunished.

In Book II of his *Republic*, Plato presents a philosophical discussion of the man who can become invisible. Socrates believed that it might be extremely unlikely for many people to remain virtuous if they could somehow become invisible. Would being invisible, we may ask, be a blessing or a curse to one who operated in such a state?

According to Plato's fable, Gyges is tending to his sheep one day when a violent thunderstorm and earthquake created a massive opening in the earth. In a state of amazement, the shepherd enters the opening and finds a hollow bronze horse with little doors. When he looks inside the horse, he sees a corpse wearing nothing other than a golden ring. Gyges takes possession of the ring and soon discovers that when he turns the collet of the ring toward himself he becomes invisible, and when he turns it outward, he becomes visible again. According to the fable, Gyges uses the ring to his advantage and, through a series of villainous deeds, usurps the king's throne.

Plato offers this story as a thought-experiment for discussion on the subject of justice. If a man could render himself invisible by so simple an act as turning the collet of his ring, would he not commit any number of unjust acts in order to achieve his own ends? In the dialogue, Glaucon argues that a man behaves justly only because he fears being caught and possibly punished. Virtue is merely a sham.

St. Ambrose, in the 4th century, commenting on Plato's story, affirmed that even if invisible, a man is nonetheless stained by his unjust acts. "The hiding place of the wise," he writes, "lies not in their hope of impunity but in his own innocency... Thus he is not recalled from sin by fear of punishment, but by the rule of a virtuous life."

H. G. Wells, influenced by Plato's "Ring of Gyges," wrote, in 1897, *The Invisible Man*. Wells portrays a man, whom he calls Griffin, who is an intense student of optics. He finds a way to reduce the refraction index of his body to the level of air so that he can neither absorb light nor reflect light. This image is not exactly scientific since the eye needs to reflect light in order to see. But Wells is weaving a fantasy and not abiding by the rules of science. Such is the nature of some science fiction. At any rate, Griffin, much to his dismay, is unable to make himself visible again. This problem occurs in Goethe's *Sorcerer's Apprentice* where the apprentice laments, "The spirits that I invoke I can no longer banish." Things do not turn out well for Griffin who becomes a madman and, in the end of the novel, is killed.

Well's "invisible man" has been performed at least a dozen times in movies as well as on TV. It has, paradoxically, been heard on the radio where the airways convey no visible personalities. Modern technology has created no end of invisible people, but in the case of the radio, the actors and listeners are invisible to each other. Nonetheless, opportunities for unvirtuous activity have been profligate.

With the computer, opportunities for theft, to center on but one example, have soared. Invisible thieves contact innocent owners of computers, convince them that their computers are malfunctioning, and then extort money from them. The problem is pandemic. Plato could not have imagined that his "ring" could be worn by millions of people. Socrates, on the other hand, warned that by rendering people invisible, immorality would flourish.

The invisible men in Well's story and in all its adaptions came to a bad end. In today's world, what can be said of those invisible thieves who bilk money from innocent and unsuspecting people? Many of them will never be brought to justice. Virtue is perfective of the person. It is not simply a social ornament nor a personal triumph. A person who lives a life that is wholly unjust is punishing himself by failing to realize what it means to be a joyous, fulfilled human being. The invisible computer thief is hurting himself more than he is hurting others. "He who steals my purse steals trash," as Shakespeare pointed out. But he who steals is, by that disreputable act, ruining his soul.

In today's highly technological world, it is easy to conceal one's infamies. What this means is that virtue must be stronger than ever because the temptations are greater than ever. The virtue of integrity gives a person the strength to be virtuous despite increasingly seductive temptations. Religion is most helpful since it brings into focus the notion that God is watching. Who am I? Am I a thief, a sneak, a coward, a dissembler, a fraud? How does one live with himself if these appellations accurately describe him? The cost to a person of unjust actions is devastatingly high. The rewards of a life of virtue are inestimable. Love of neighbor demands justice to him. A person, in communicating with others through modern technologies, should behave in the same way as if he were visible to them. There are, indeed, disadvantages to being invisible.

Mercy

Charting the Mercy of God

There is a branch of sociology consisting of self-appointed scientists who are committed to environmental determinism. They believe that the environment in which one is raised accurately predicts his future. A dark environment for the young produces a dark environment for the adult. Only a bright environment will produce a bright future. These environmental determinists know nothing of either God's grace or heroic virtue. They cleave to the fallacy that social conditioning rules the world.

Let us follow the life of one particular soul, of many, who escaped the net that environmental determinists had prepared for him. He was one of eight children born to improvident and impecunious parents who sought to improve their bleak financial situation by purchasing a large house that was to be used as a school for young ladies. Not a single student ever darkened their doorstep. The family's small, well-fingered collection of books was sold. Our protagonist was sent to the pawnbroker with teaspoons, silver teapots, and other small articles that fetched a few shillings. Little by little, the household furniture disappeared leaving only a kitchen table, a few chairs, and the beds. The bedraggled father could not pay what he owed and was sent to debtor's prison.

In order to ease the family's impoverished state, our leading character, barely 12 years old at the time, was forced to leave school and work at a boot-blacking factory for 6 shillings a week. There, he labored from eight in the morning until eight at night, Monday through Saturday, wrapping and labelling pots of paste-blacking for boots and fire-grates.

The warehouse where he worked was a tumble-down building, odorous with dirt and decay. Rats scurried across its rotted floors and dank cellars. What was even more disturbing to our young gentleman was the miserable way he was treated by his co-workers. In reflecting on this dark period later on in his life, he lamented that he had "No advice, no counsel, no consolation, from anyone that I can call to mind" and added that "but for the mercy of God, I might easily have been, for any care that was taken of me, a little robber or a little vagabond." He had hit on the right phrase, "the mercy of God," the unexpected intervention of God's care which made all the difference in the world. His tenure at the dilapidated warehouse lasted no more than four or five months. But its effect on him lasted a lifetime.

His fortune improved when his father received a family inheritance that was used to pay off his debts. Much to his relief, our hero was permitted to go back to school. The good times, however, did not last very long. Once again, when he was 15, he was forced to drop out of school and work as an office boy to contribute to his family's income.

What became of this young man who could find "No words to express the agony of my soul?" Well, he found many words to become the greatest English novelist of the Victorian Age. His name appears in G. K. Chesterton's tribute to him: *Charles Dickens, The Last of the Great Men.* "If he learnt to whitewash the universe, it was in a blacking factory that he learnt it."

Edgar Johnson, author of *Charles Dickens: His Tragedy and Triumph*, states that "the blacking house that made him a man of insuperable resolve and deadly determination, also made him [Dickens] for life a sympathizer with all suffering and with all victims of injustice." In another study of Dickens, Norman and Jeanne MacKenzie agree that this dark, seemingly hopeless period, "had forged an indissoluble bond of sympathy, even of identity, with the homeless, the friendless, the orphans, the hungry, the uneducated, and even the prisoners of London's lower depth."

Dickens transmuted the tribulations that impressed themselves so deeply when he was young into the immortal characters he created in his novels. He helped to destroy certain unjust institutions in England. And he did it with his pen, merely by describing them. His sympathy for all human beings allowed him to spark a social justice revolution without losing sight of the inherent dignity of each person. On the one hand, his writings seem to say, "Defeat poverty; on the other hand, they were fully in accord with Christ's beatitude, "Blessed are the poor." He was urging improvement in social conditions of the working class while at the same time showing that the Crachits, despite their poverty, were happy, and Scrooge, despite his wealth, was the picture of misery. With Dickens in mind, G. K. Chesterton remarked that, "There is a great man who makes every man feel small. But the real great man is the one who makes every man feel great."

Charles Dickens left us, thanks to the mercy of God, with no short supply of moral wisdom: "No one is useless in this world who lightens the burden of it to anyone else." "Charity begins at home and justice begins next door." "Have a heart that never hardens, and a temper that never tires, and a touch that never hurts." "There are dark shadows on the earth, but its lights are stronger in the contrast." "I will honor Christmas in my heart, and try to keep it all the year."

Dickens' life may offer more inspiration than any of the novels he penned.

Fidelity

Can there be a Replacement for Religion?

Sigmund Freud (1856-1930) is a paradox. He is the analyst who himself invites analysis. He is a scientist but wanted more than science could offer him. He wanted to be a revolutionary. "I will move all hell," he wrote (*Acheronta movebo*). As a consequence, he added a certain mythology (the Oedipus complex, Electra complex, and so on) to his world view in order to broaden his intellectual horizon. Therefore, he bequeathed to the world two radically incompatible and antagonistic elements.

His attitude toward religion is also ambiguous. On the one hand, because he did not believe in the reality of the spiritual, he reduced the human being to a purely materialistic entity. Belief in the fatherhood of God, according to Freud, is projecting the father image onto the sky. Holy Communion is "oral introjection." It is derived, allegedly, from the primitive state of mankind, when cannibalistic ceremonies were practiced. In general, for Sigmund Freud, religion is a "neurosis."

His often quoted phrase, "Anatomy is destiny" has attracted strong criticism since it leaves man without freedom. Nonetheless, this materialistic view is an essential part of Freud's view of man. "People do not really want freedom," he writes, "because freedom involves responsibility and most people are frightened of responsibility." His materialistic view of man inevitably leads to one that is pessimistic: "I have found little that is 'good' about human beings on the whole. In my experience most of them are trash, no matter whether they publicly subscribe to this or that ethical doctrine or to none at all. That is something that you cannot say aloud, or perhaps even think."

Freud's pessimism was not confined to humans: "Yes, America is gigantic, but a gigantic mistake." Life is too hard for people. As a result, they need comforting illusions and cannot dispense with "intoxicating media in the struggle for happiness and in keeping misery at a distance." He maintained that history is nothing more than new people making the same old mistakes. On the other hand, "Time spent with cats is never wasted."

Freud died at 83 years of age, of a lethal dose of morphine administered at his request by his friend and physician. His last words were, "Now it is nothing but torture and makes no sense anymore."

Freud's antipathy toward religion could hardly be more extreme. And yet, he held that the teachings of religion are indispensable and irreplaceable. How is this seemingly contradictory stance possible?

Freud, himself, dealt with the question concerning the value of religion. He resolved the problem in his own mind by separating the teachings of religion from their spiritual component. He understood that education is needed in order to preserve civilization and keep it from descending into chaos. But what should be its content." In *The Future of an Illusion*, he makes the case for religious doctrines as advantageous to civilization, "For it allows a refinement and sublimation of ideas, which make it possible for it to be divested of most of the traces which it bears of primitive and infantile thinking." Since society is obliged to offer children an education that is worthwhile, "it seems to me," Freud writes, "that the religious is by far the most suitable for the purpose."

Religion in itself may be an illusion for Freud, but religion cannot be replaced entirely: "If men are taught that there is no almighty and all-just God, no divine world-order and no future life, they will feel exempt from all obligation to obey the precepts of civilization. Everyone will, without inhibition or fear, follow his asocial, egoistic instincts and seek to exercise his power; Chaos . . . will come again" (*The Future of an Illusion*, p. 34).

Freud fails to deal with a most important question. Why is it that something artificial (religious doctrine without religion) is the most suitable factor in safeguarding civilization against falling into Chaos? How can something so artificial be so natural?" To answer Freud is to point out that the affinity that religious doctrine has for man is because it is truly natural, which is to say, that it is not something that is imposed on man but something that springs from his very nature as a being created by God and made to serve him. As St. Augustine famously states, "Our hearts are made for Thee and shall not rest until they rest in Thee."

Religious doctrine cannot exist without religion. It is not something that is invented. It came about because of religion. Freud takes milk from the cow and then denies that cows exist. The impulse to be religious is born in the hearts of men. And it has been placed there by the God who created them.

Because Freud could not affirm that it is in the nature of man to seek God, he could not begin to understand the workings of grace. Hence, his pessimism was unredeemable. He did, however, and despite himself, offer an argument that religion is really irreplaceable.

When religious doctrines are obeyed, the spirituality of their religious foundation arrives along with them. One cannot live in accordance with religious doctrine without drinking from the cup in which they rest. And that cup, which contains the religious doctrine, is religion itself, spiritualized and conveying the reality of a loving God. Freud has bequeathed to us more than he thought. He has given us a strong argument that religion cannot be replaced.

Hope

Clarifying Two Meanings of Hope

We are inescapably creatures of the future. This is why we live in hope. We need a reason to get up in the morning. But there are two radically different kinds of hope. It is important that we understand how they are different and how they relate to each other. To the first, we may assign the word, "immediate." We use this word on a daily basis. We hope it will not rain tomorrow. We hope our team will win. We hope you are feeling better. This kind of hope is not far removed from wish. Nonetheless, it carries us forward and gives added meaning to tomorrow. It is ephemeral, however, since every hope fulfilled is replaced by a hope yet to be fulfilled. We live from one hope to another and learn that none of our hopes has lasting satisfaction.

To the second kind of hope, we may assign the word, "eternal." This is the hope that does not disappear and is irreplaceable. It is the hope that survives when all the day-to-day hopes are fulfilled. It is the hope that characterizes us as persons and is inseparable from us. It is like a barnacle attached to its host. As the author of *Moby Dick* has said, "Hope proves man deathless. It is the struggle of the soul, breaking loose from what is perishable and attesting her eternity."

In Shakespeare's *Henry VIII*, Cardinal Wolsey looks back on his life and recalls his youth "when to-day he puts forth tender leaves of hope; tomorrow's blossoms." But for Wolsey, hope does not spring eternal. In his old age, at the end of a wasted political career, he finds himself in a state of despair: "And when he falls, he falls like Lucifer, never to hope again" (Act III, scene 2, line 24). There are no more tragic words than these.

At the entrance of Hell, inscribed in dim colors above the doorway's lofty arch, appeared a sentence that caused Dante to shudder. Turning to his guide, the Roman poet, Virgil, he said, "Master, these words import hard meaning." Hard meaning, indeed! "Abandon hope, ye who enter here." These words express the very essence of Hell—life without hope (*The Divine Comedy,* "Inferno," Canto 3: (*Lasciate ogni speranza voi ch'entrate*).

To be in Hell is to be without hope. The reverse of this statement is also true: to be without hope is to be in Hell. Despair is a condition that many experience when they have lost the hope that gives their lives an overriding significance. Pursuing our immediate hopes can distract us from the realization of our eternal hope. We were created to be with God. The baubles we pick up along the way are not lasting. Eternal hope transcends immediate hope.

Life is a journey, and eternal hope is our North Star. Therefore, it is appropriate that we are called "pilgrims," "wayfarers," "journeyman," and "*homo viator.*" Hope is always with us while we continue to travel toward it.

Early in his pontificate, John Paul II acquired the nickname, "His Polishness the Hope." He was the virtual embodiment of hope. It was fitting, then, that George Weigel titled his definitive biography of His Holiness, *Witness to Hope.* When John Paul addressed the United Nations in 1995, he dared to present himself as a "witness to hope" despite the fact that he spoke these words at the end of a century known for unprecedented wickedness.

Hope: Clarifying Two Meanings of Hope

As the third millennium was approaching, the Holy Father stated that "Christians are called to prepare for the Great Jubilee of the beginning of the Third Millennium *by renewing their hope in the definitive coming of the Kingdom of God,* preparing for it daily in their hearts, in the Christian community to which they belong, in their particular social context, and in world history." This hope is not the hope of secular humanism. Nor is it the hope of a materialist way of life. It is an eternal hope that is related to Christ and His Kingdom.

Pope Benedict XVI continued the work of John Paul II in stressing the essential importance of hope. In his 2007 book *Saved by Hope* (*Spe Salvi*), he warns that too much emphasis on satisfying the immediate hopes can cause a person to lose eternal hope: "Yet our daily efforts in pursuing our own lives and in working for the world's future either tire us or turn into fanaticism, unless we are enlightened by the radiance of the great hope that cannot be destroyed even by small-scale failures or by a breakdown in matters of historic importance." We cannot build the Kingdom of God by our own efforts. We should understand that our immediate hopes should be set within the context of our eternal hope.

As we journey through life mindful of our eternal hope, our choices and actions are placed in order. Consequently, our eternal hope has an important influence on our immediate hopes. We should not want to live in a disordered way as if our earthly pilgrimage is inconsistent with our ultimate hope. Our eternal hope confers importance on selecting our immediate hopes wisely. The two hopes are coordinated in the same way as heaven and earth.

We are saved by hope when we align our daily decisions to that ultimate hope which leads us to God and the heaven that he has prepared for us.

Resourcefulness

On Overcoming Laziness

The celebrated novelist Somerset Maugham said there were two keys to his success as a writer: getting up in the morning and going to bed at night. By virtue of this strategy, he defeated laziness twice, by overcoming laziness in the morning and retiring at the proper time so that he would be ready to rise the next day.

We are all saddled with chronic laziness. *E dolce far niente* (it is sweet to do nothing), say the Italians. The Spanish go one step further and say, "It is sweet to do nothing and then rest afterwards." We are all, at one time or another, deserving of the epithet, "lazy-bones." And a "lazy good-for-nothing" is a virtual condemnation.

People look forward to the summer when being lazy becomes respectable. Or they may prefer the term "indolent," which seems to raise laziness to a higher level. Nonetheless, no one is proud of being lazy and comes to regret the oceans of time that were unproductive. There are no rewards for laziness. On the other hand, laziness in not doing anything is not a crime. Yet, it may be a terrible fault.

St. Thomas Aquinas treated laziness under the term *acedia*. It is "sorrow over . . . an internal and divine good [in us] (*ST II-II*, q. 35, a, 2). It is, for Aquinas, a sin against charity since it fails to accept "friendship with God" and "the spiritual life that dwells within us." The Angelic Doctor in this instance is referring to spiritual laziness, the most pernicious kind.

What he is saying is that God has endowed us with certain gifts (or talents). These gifts are to be used and developed as a form of gratitude. God wants us to appreciate the gifts He has given us and wants us to experience the joy that results when we put our gifts into practice. It is both unappreciative as well as irresponsible to allow these gifts to lie fallow. Therefore, spiritual laziness (*acedia*) is a sin against God. It is also a sin, though not as grievous, against others since it deprives them of enjoying the fruits of our labor.

In *ST I*, Aquinas stated that *acedia* "is a kind of sadness, whereby one becomes sluggish in spiritual exercises because they weary the body." Here, he is offering a direct paraphrase of St. Augustine's own definition of the vice.

God is not asking us to do more than we can. He does not want to overburden us. With this in mind, we read Matthew 11:28-30 with greater understanding: "Come all you who are weary and burdened, and I will give you rest. Take my yoke upon you, and learn from me, for I am gentle and humble of heart, and you will find rest for your souls. For my yoke is easy and my burden light."

Spiritual laziness, then, is our resistance to participating in the divine nature, to our friendship with God. It is a resistance to the burdens of commitment involved in that relationship. It is the preference to do nothing rather than to accept and cultivate the gifts that God has given us.

Spiritual laziness is hard to excuse. British novelist Anthony Burgess puts things into perspective when he remarks: "Wedged as we are between two eternities of idleness, there is no excuse for being idle now." In the words of the American poet, John Greenleaf Whittier, "For of all sad words of tongue or pen, the saddest are these: 'It might have been!'" A person lives once and cannot go back and rectify his past mistakes. The dividends of laziness are sorrow and regret.

We are created by God but come from nothing. Therefore, there is a profound tendency for us to slip back into that eternal void from which we were rescued by God. We are caught in the pincers between grace and gravity. Laziness is surrendering to the gravitational impulse. God bids us to follow the path of grace. The mind is like a clock that is running down and continually needs to be rewound. We need inspiration to overcome laziness in addition to appreciating the gifts God has granted us.

Bishop Sheen has said that "Mental laziness, above all, manifests itself in skepticism or the certitude that nothing is certain. The uncommitted mind is lazy because it never closes on anything." It is a tragedy that moral issues of critical importance are lazily resolved by a single word. For abortion it is "choice," for pornography it is "pleasure," for euthanasia it is "dignity," and for divorce it is "convenience." The lazy mind is a danger to all humanity.

Some time ago when Dean Martin was about to retire from show business, he was asked what he planned to do in his retirement. "I plan to get pleasantly stoned each day," was his response. The popular crooner was not being candid. He was pandering to an image the media had created for him and one that would please his legion of fans who admired the individual who could shed all responsibilities and just do what he wanted to do.

How, then, do we overcome laziness? We should be inspired by the energy of others who have left their wisdom in books, music, and various other arts. We should remind ourselves that God has given us talents, no matter how modest, that He wants us to develop. In this regard, we have been commissioned by God. Our future will be happier if we put into practice today what God has given us for a lifetime.

Authenticity

The Dethronement of Man

Hamlet paints a panegyric to man when he declares "how noble he is in reason! how infinite in faculty! in form and moving how express and admirable! in action how like an angel! in apprehension how like a god! the beauty of the world! the paragon of animals! (Act 2, scene 2).

Does this lofty description of the human being accord with reality? It did in Shakespeare's time, but that was the 16th and early 17th centuries. Various intellectuals of the modern world have taken man apart piece by piece, diminished and dethroned him.

Is man noble in reason? For Sigmund Freud, the answer is an emphatic "no." For the celebrated Austrian psychologist, man is dominated by his unconscious. He is an "ego" dominated by an "id." He is "discontent" and prostrates himself before "illusions." There is very little that is noble about man. "Life," he writes in *Civilization and its Discontents*, "as we find it, is too hard for us; it brings us too many pains, disappointments and impossible tasks. In order to bear it we cannot dispense with palliative measures."

Is man infinite in faculty? Aristotle said that man's mind can know all things. He knew something about the spiritual nature of man. David Hume argues that we should not trust "the fallacious deductions of our reason." His skepticism is the polar opposite of the confidence philosophers had in knowing all things from Aristotle through the Middle Ages.

Is man admirable in form and moving? Man is named *Homo erectus* because he stands on two feet. This is a noble stance. He has an opposable thumb which allows him to use tools and build cities. His admirable movements are displayed in the ballet and in sports. Nonetheless, transhumanists want to transform through bio-engineering into a different species. Transhumanist Ray Kurzweil, in his book *The Age of Spiritual Machines*, predicted that "[t]he 21st century will be different. The human species, along with the computational technology it created, will be able to solve age-old problems … and will be in a position to change the nature of mortality in a post-biological future." Most transhumanists are atheists who are attempting to construct God.

Is man like an angel in his actions? Here, Shakespeare is alluding to how man comforts and aids others in times of trouble. "Please be an angel and help him," people are wont to say. For Jean-Paul Sartre, helping others diminishes my individuality. Friedrich Nietzsche regarded moral virtues as holding back the emergence of the superman (*unber mensch*). Materialist philosophers deny that humans could act as angels since angels did not exist.

Can man apprehend like a God? Christian theology contends that man, being endowed with reason, was created in the image of God. The wave of atheists in the modern world beginning with Arthur Schopenhauer, by denying the existence of God, denied that man could imitate a non-existent God in any way. The Psalmist posed an unanswerable question when he asked, "What is man that God is mindful of him?" For Hegel, man thinks in contradictions, moving from thesis to antithesis. Marx adopted this way of thinking as he framed man in a dialectic that evolved historically.

Authenticity: The Dethronement of Man

Is man the beauty of the world? Shakespeare, in his panegyric, also refers to man as the quintessence of dust. The word "quintessence" has an interesting etymology. It is derived from two Latin terms, *quinta* (the fifth) and *essentia* (essence). For the ancient Greeks, the four elements—air, earth, fire, and water—were perishable, but the fifth essence was imperishable. Man was fashioned from dust and attained the highest and most beautiful form in the world. For Jean-Paul Sartre, however, man is "a useless passion." "We should regard every man," Schopenhauer advises us, "first and foremost a being who exists only as a consequence of his culpability and whose life is an expiation of the crime of being born."

Is man the paragon of animals? Charles Darwin's evolutionary philosophy views man as a descendent of primates. As evolution continues, however, something higher than man might appear on the stage of life. Man is not the paragon of animals, but just another animal. He is a creature who has evolved by chance. Darwin contends that, "If . . . men were reared under precisely that same conditions as hive-bees, there can hardly be a doubt that our unmarried females would, like the worker-bees, think it a sacred duty to kill their brothers, and mothers would strive to kill their female daughters; and no one would think of interfering."

Modern man has been subject to the battering and bruising on each of the seven levels that Shakespeare found praiseworthy. Not only has he been dethroned, but he has also been reduced to a mockery of his former self, a struggling animal trapped in a godless and hostile world who cannot rely on what his reason tells him and whose suffering is the painful price of the crime of existing

Catholic psychiatrist Karl Stern, in his book *The Third Revolution*, offers of similarly dismal portrait of how modern man has been dethroned: "Look at what has happened to the Christian within four centuries. First he is evicted from the geocentric cosmos. Then he is told that his higher achievements are accidental by-products of the fight for food. Then he is demoted to the position of a cousin in the monkey family. And finally his reason is declared to be a precariously fragile something determined by forces the very nature of which are obscure to him."

The Christian must make a supreme effort in the present world to recapture his true identity. He is a child of God, a noble, intelligent creature whose destiny is to love and be loved, to know and to serve, as he makes his journey back to God. Many of our intellectuals have failed us, grossly misrepresenting us as a travesty of who we really are. We do have at our disposal the Church that has consistently taught that man is created in the image and likeness of God.

Belief

Clarifying Two Kinds of Belief

There are two radically different kinds of belief. One is the willingness to belief without sufficient investigation. It is a form of belief that is not supported by reason. People who are gullible or superstitious fall into this category. On the other hand, there is belief that is indeed supported by reason and is affirmed by investigation. It is of great practical significance that we distinguish these two types of belief.

On the evening of October 30, 1938, Orson Wells directed and narrated a radio production of H. G. Wells' novel, *War of the Worlds*. A significant number of listeners believed the broadcast was delivering terrifying news. The headlines the next day in the *New York Times* read as follows: "Radio listeners in panic, taking war drama as fact. Many flee homes to escape 'Gas Raid from Mars'—Phone calls swamp police at broadcast of Wells fantasy." This was an example of belief turned to hysteria.

To celebrate April 1, Burger King offered hamburgers for left-handed people that were carefully rotated to the left. A surprising number of customers requested this special April Fools Day treat. There are still members of the flat Earth Society. It is bad luck to open an umbrella indoors and breaking a mirror brings 7 years of bad luck. Entering a house leading with the left foot is a bad omen. Man is easily misled.

I gave a talk in Delaware one time and had my audience believe that their state was originally founded by an intrepid, though uncredited, navigator from Sweden names Loof Lirpa. My listeners began to laugh, but only when I told them that he brought with him IKEA furniture and Swedish meatballs, and that his name was April Fool in reverse.

We are all prone to believe in things that lack rational support. This is evident in how people are easily persuaded by television commercials or eagerly taken in by political promises. At the same time, they are slow to believe the truths of the Catholic Church. That the Church has always connected faith with reason is evidenced by the fact that the Church founded universities and has always championed the role of reason in education. In my own case, my theology text was entitled *Reasons for Our Faith*.

Are there reasons for believing in the truths of the Catholic Church? Why should we choose this Church and no other? Bishop Sheen offered three reasons: 1) The historical fact that Christ was preannounced for centuries; 2) The fact of miracles as the guarantee of His mission from God; 3) The agreement of His message with right reason and the aspirations of the human heart. Sheen argues that faith extends reason just as the telescope extends the eye. Faith, which is to say, what we believe, enlarges our vision. "Once we have faith," he writes, "new dimensions of knowledge and new areas of wisdom are opened up which before were never disclosed."

Pope John Paul II gave special attention to the relationship between faith and reason in his Encyclical Letter, *Fides et Ratio*. He begins by offering the world a memorable phrase: "Faith and reason are like two wings on which the human spirit rises to the contemplation of truth; and God has placed in the human heart a desire to know the truth—in a word, to know himself—so that, by knowing and loving God, men and women may also come to the fullness of truth about themselves."

The Catholic faith rests on a dynamic and reciprocal relationship between Sacred Tradition, Sacred Scripture, and the Magisterium of the Church. None of these three can survive without the others.

Credulity and superstition have proven to be disappointing often enough so that a disbelief in belief in general has risen. But not all belief is deceptive. Once united with reason, as well as personal experience and tradition, belief becomes credible, as it is for Catholic faith.

The impressive gains in science have led many to believe that science does not need faith, that it will ultimately penetrate all the secrets of the universe. There are two problems, however, with this view. One is that scientists need to have faith that the mind of man can grasp the principles of the universe. Reason itself cannot explain how the microcosm of man's mind became attuned to the macrocosm of the world around him. As Einstein put it, that the universe is comprehensible is itself incomprehensible. The second reason has to do with the inherent limitations of reason. Science has made it increasingly clear, given the indeterminacy principle and other formidable obstacles, that reason can go only so far in its exploration of the world. There are realities that we need to know that reason cannot discover. Theology is still needed.

The distinguished American astronomer Robert Jastrow has made the point with a dash of humor: "For the scientist who has lived by his faith in the power of reason, the story ends like a bad dream.

He has scaled the mountains of ignorance, he is about to conquer the highest peak; as he pulls himself over the final rock, he is greeted by a band of theologians who have been sitting there for centuries."

Belief without reason is a blind alley. Reason without faith is severely limited. Neither rationalism nor fideism are satisfactory. Together, they open many doors that were formerly closed. United, reason and faith harmonize two yearnings that arise from the heart that help us to know who we are and where we are going.

Neighborliness

The Central Problem in Life

At a conference in Fribourg, Switzerland, in 1975, Karol Wojtyla (later Pope John Paul II) stated, "The central problem of life for humanity in our times, perhaps in all times, is this: *participation or alienation*. This problem seems to take on sharper contours today. It is also one that is very much alive in people's minds."

Wojtyla was not one for exaggerating. At the same time, his words cry out for a fuller explanation. We should know more clearly about this central problem in life so that we can do something about it.

Wojtyla begins by calling attention to the "*I*." This is something we all know in a direct way. The "*I*" is my conscious self who looks out at the world according to my own unique perspective. It is I who dreams, hopes, suffers, and fears. To myself, I am supremely important. It is I who thinks, knows, and philosophizes. I am a mystery to myself, but I persist in maintaining my unique outlook on life. I am a human being.

Secondly, I notice that each person of the many whom I encounter on a daily basis are also human beings who think and act from the vantage point of their own "I." I live in a community, but I should think of others not merely as members of a community, but as *neighbors*. This is a most important distinction. When I recognize my neighbor as being, like myself, another "*I*," I begin to participate in his humanity. As Wojtyla states: "As human beings, we are capable of participation in the very humanity of other people, and because of this, every human being can be our *neighbor*." Participation arises when we become aware that the other person is another "*I*" like ourselves.

It is a simple matter to see other people as merely other people and not as having a center of consciousness (their own "*I*"). In this regard, we see people as less than who they are and are unjust to them. This is alienation which, essentially, is the negation of participation.

The most extreme expression of alienation between people is found in Jean-Paul Sartre's play *No Exit*, where one of his characters declares, "Hell is other people" (*L'enfer c'est les autres*). These words also capture the moral philosophy of the French existentialist. Other people, for Sartre, impinge on my freedom. Such an outlook prohibits community, even a community of strangers.

There are less severe forms of alienation when people simply fail to affirm the other's humanity. Lady Diana Cooper, a wealthy socialite, once remarked, "I do think servants should not be ill. We have quite enough illness ourselves without them adding to the symptoms." Snobbery rests on alienation and is not attractive. No doubt Lady Cooper's superciliousness was not accepted by her servants. As G. K. Chesterton once remarked, "People who look down on other people don't end up being looked up to." Chesterton made the same point much stronger when he said of Charles Dickens that "he disliked a certain look on the face of a man when he looked down on another man. And that look on the face is, indeed, the only thing in the world that we have really to fight between here and the fires of Hell."

Alienation can lead to slavery. Participation can lead to friendship. Wojtyla is not exaggerating in the least when he says that the question of participation or alienation is the central problem of life.

This problem is exacerbated in our present world by structures of alienation. The myriad of automobiles that clog the highway are images of alienation, the parties of each car, being separated from every other car. People are alienated from their co-travellers while they listen to the radio.

I once gave a lecture on the structure of alienation to my philosophy students. I did not want my words to remain merely words, so I asked them to counter an example of alienation that they found in their life and then report on it. Since I wanted to put into practice what I preached, I was presented with an opportunity on my way home. I had to pick up something from the grocery store and noticed that cashiers were not looking at their customers; rather, they were preoccupied with the groceries and the cash register. I noticed that a price tag was stuck to my cashier's hair. I paused and wondered if it would be embarrassing to point this out to her. Then I thought how more embarrassed she would be when she got home and realized she was wearing this sticker all day without anybody pointing it out to her. What would they think? Wearing a price tag on your head lends to no end of jokes. And so, I pointed out her mild dilemma in as diplomatic a way I knew. It all went very well, and we had a good laugh. Overcoming alienation invites neighborly interactions.

We are all human and we all look out at the world from our "I." From this awareness of universal kinship, we can participate in the humanity of our neighbor. This is a ground level issue. How we evaluate and treat each other is, indeed, the fundamental issue in life. As Karol Wojtyla concludes, "Participation signifies a basic personalization of the relationship of one human being to another." How much, for all mankind, is this devoutly to be desired!

Faith

What Is the Moon Saying?

"Let there be light" is such a powerful and memorable phrase that it dwarfs what *Genesis 1:16* states shortly thereafter concerning the creation of the moon. It is appropriate, then, that Monday should follow Sunday. The moon follows the sun as the night follows the day: "And God made the two great lights—the greater light to rule the day and the lesser light to rule the night..." *Psalm 104:19* informs us that "He made the moon to mark the seasons." According to scientists, the moon was formed 4.51 billion years ago after the earth's formation. It has been orbiting ever since, a tribute to the constancy of the cosmos.

We cannot look directly at the sun without being blinded, but the soft glow of the moon is relaxing. Ancient watchers of the sky were fascinated by the moon's cycles and how it changed position and shape before it disappeared from the sky only to return again. It repeated this cycle over a period of 29 days. This allowed people to count the days and predict the arrival of the seasons. Its period, being roughly a month, is the basis for its name.

The waxing and waning of the moon symbolizes the fickle nature of man, his changing heart, and lack of constancy. The sun, by contrast, is immobile. The sun is 92 million miles from the earth, while the moon is its neighbor, a mere 250,000 miles away, close enough to occupy. The sun and moon attest to the diversity of God's creation.

The fact that the lunar cycle is nearly a month corresponds to a woman's menstrual cycle. It was once believed that if a woman merely looked at a full moon, she became pregnant. On the other hand, a person adversely affected by the moon could become a lunatic. Werewolves, according to folklore, came out during a full moon. The moon influenced men, women, and the tides in different ways. The word, "month" is derived from the word "moon."

The moon is the middle ground between the light of the sun and the darkness of the night. Hence, some people believed that it represents the realm between the conscious and the unconscious. It affects the earth in many ways, not only the tides, but the rains, the waters, and the seasons. And its gravity keeps the earth rotating on its proper tilt.

A professor of engineering, a victim of the technological imperative, once said that since we now have the technology, we should blow up the moon. The destruction of the moon would be catastrophic. The moon is far more than a pleasant object in the sky at night. It is a ruler. Getting rid of the moon would be akin to assassinating a king.

The moon shows the earth the same face. How the moon appears on its other face remains a mystery. Nonetheless, the pock-marked face that seemingly looks at us smiles on lovers. Hence, the endless number of songs that include the moon in its title: Moon River, Fly Me to the Moon, Moonlight and Roses, Moonlight Becomes You, Moon over Miami, Blue Moon, Moon Dreams, Moonglow, Racing with the Moon, Lazy Moon and Moonglow. And we should not forget Glenn Miller's Moonlight Serenade (he also composed Moonlight Cocktail) or Beethoven's Moonlight Sonata. A theme from

Faith: What is the Moon Saying?

Rachmaninoff's Second Piano Concerto became the popular tune, Full Moon and Empty Arms. A full moon plays Cupid from a distance. It warms the heart. People become amorous when they are "moonstruck," the title of a movie that features the most outrageous musical introduction sung by Dean Martin: "When the moon hits your eye like a big pizza pie, that's amore." On a loftier level of poetry, Edgar Allan Poe wrote, "For the moon never beams without sending me dreams."

Moonshine is made at night under the light of the moon. But, also, people love to spoon under the light of the silvery moon. Moonlight is far more romantic than sunlight. It lifts the lid of both prohibition and inhibition. Poetess Maggie Dewane said, "Let's dance together on moonbeams. On this cool spring eve. The nights are young. And ready for teasing. There's mischief in the night air."

A "blue moon" is the second full moon that appears within the same calendar month. This occurs every thirty-two months, virtually a month of months. Hence, the phrase "once in a blue moon," referring to something that happens rarely.

For Christianity, the moon is symbol of faith. This is because we need a light in our darkest moments. The moon lightens our path when our vision is limited. It saves the night from complete invisibility. There are times when we see so little that faith is the only thing that will guide us.

What is the moon saying to us? Have faith! Know that faith has its own light. And though it may seem dim, it can offer us a better way of navigating through life than what we can see in the light of day. The moon, as does the sun, proclaims the glory of God.

We might imagine the moon in terms of the three supernatural virtues: faith, hope, and love. Moonglow lights our path and represents the faith we live by. Moonshine is what we see when we look at the face of the moon reflecting the sun, stirring our hope to be with God. Moonbeams are the currents of love that the moon sends our way.

Reverence

What are the Stars Saying?

A famous and well-known nursery rhyme is sung to the words, "Twinkle, twinkle little star, how I wonder what you are! Up above the world so high, like a diamond in the sky." The lyrics are from an early nineteenth century English poem written by Jane Taylor. The tune, a French melody, *Ah vous dirai-je, Maman* (Oh! Shall I tell you, Mommy?) was first published in 1761 and set to twelve variations by none other than Wolfgang Amadeus Mozart. It has a charmed history.

The rhyme is fascinating insofar as it unites extremes. The star is "little" to our eyes, and even more so to the eyes of a child. As adults, however, we know that science teaches us the stars are gigantic, much larger than we can possibly imagine. In addition, another extreme is introduced, namely, that between the location of the star (up high) and its comparison with a diamond which is found deep below the earth. It is a paradox, holding together its opposites. And a paradox that applies to the adult who keeps his eyes on the stars but his feet on the ground. The star also elicits wonder, which is the beginning of wisdom.

Is there anything more fascinating and yet more adaptable than a star? A sheriff wears one. Several sports teams have adopted the star as their emblem. Players aspire to be stars and showcase their talents in an All Star game. Stars populate the American flag. We wish upon stars and find them in a lover's eyes. We hitch our wagons to them. They characterize the accomplished celebrity and are presented in miniature to heroes. Texas has one, but only one. A dreamer is starry-eyed and hopes to find stardom. One may be born under a lucky star, but coming into the world on the wrong side of a star proves disaster. A single star tops the Christmas tree. And the Magi, we cannot forget, followed a star. Stars are rich in symbolism, but they are also profound in implication.

What are the stars saying to us? Philosopher Immanuel Kant was most fascinated by two things that seemed infinitely apart: "the stars above and the moral law within." They spoke to David. In Psalm 19:1, he states, "The heavens declare the glory of God; the skies proclaim the work of his hands." When we look toward the heavens, we see stars. The glory of the stars, however, is not in themselves, but in what they are saying—that they have been created by God.

Étienne Gilson, in addition to being a world-class historian, is an excellent philosopher. He finds that *coeli enarrant gloriam Dei* (the heavens declare the glory of God) have inspired both St. Augustine and St. Thomas Aquinas because in some way they bear His likeness. "With St. Thomas," Gilson writes, "the divine likeness sinks for the first time into the heart of nature, goes down beyond order, number and beauty, and touches the very efficacy of causality." God cannot create a world that does not bear in some way the imprint of His authorship. When we see the greatness of the work, we sense the greatness of the workman. God's signature is in everything he creates.

The affinity the stars have for the divinity was recognized by Vincent van Gogh when he said, "When I have a terrible need of—shall I say the word—religion, then I go out and paint the stars."

Reverence: What are the Stars Saying?

Shakespeare referred to stars as "These blessed candles of the night." They decorate an invisible altar behind which is a priestly God. There is something inescapably religious about the sky's canopy of stars.

Stars come out at night. "Stars were not stars unless they met the black," wrote the poet Don Marquis. They arrive just when we need them, to provide hope and consolation after the day's hard labor. In order for them to shine, the sun must set, and the sky must darken. So, too, hope can arrive when our outlook is bleak or when we suffer a loss.

Astronomers tell us, "A star is any massive self-luminous celestial body of gas that shines by radiation derived from its internal energy sources." That is scientifically correct, but that is not what the stars are telling us. They are telling us that they are ambassadors of God and signs of encouragement and hope. They fill us with a wonder that leads us to discover more about God's creation. They speak to our heart, our poetic side, for they are, as Byron declared, "the poetry of heaven." G. K. Chesterton heard what the stars were saying and encapsulated his understanding in the following sentence: "If seeds in the black earth can turn into such beautiful roses, what might not the heart of man become in his long journey toward the stars?"

Life is a journey. Man is made in the image of God. Roses are beautiful, but not as glorious as is the heart of man. We can hardly imagine what great things God has in mind for us as we make our pilgrimage toward God. The starry night is a spectacle that touches everyone. We look to the stars for guidance, hope, and inspiration. They will not fail us. "The stars," as the poet John Milton has reminded us, "that nature hung in heaven, and filled their lamps with everlasting oil, give due light to the misled and lonely traveller."

Love

What neither Plato nor Aristotle Realized

The intellectual world remains in awe concerning the philosophical brilliance of Plato and Aristotle. As a tribute to their excellence, Raphael astutely positions them in the center of his masterpiece, *The School of Athens*. Aristotle is depicted holding his treatise on ethics and thrusting his arm outwardly indicating that his primary concern is human beings and how they interact with each other. Plato is shown holding his book on the formation of the universe, *Timaeus*, and pointing upward toward the sky, indicating that truth is to be found in higher forms. Together, Plato and Aristotle complement each other. The breadth of their combined thought covers both this world and one that is higher. Their view is comprehensive. Their influence, given the range of their thought, from politics to poetry, from motion to metaphysics, is unparalleled.

Nonetheless, something escaped them, something far too unbelievable for either Plato or Aristotle to comprehend. It is a love that can span the infinite distance that separates God from man. How is such an unlikely phenomenon possible? Revelation tells us that God created man. But not only that, but He created man in his own likeness. Furthermore, He sent His only begotten Son to express His divine love by dying on the Cross for all mankind. Christianity is so implausible, as C. S. Lewis remarked, that it is "uninventible." And yet it is true!

There is no word in the English language that has as many applications as the word "love." "I love coffee," "I love tea," "I love a Gershwin tune," I love a rainy day," "I love eating out," "I love to trick people," "I love throwing caution to the wind." In this verbal whirlwind, how do we understand the meaning of this elusive word?

We may distinguish three levels of meaning for the word "love." The Greeks spoke of *eros, philia,* and *agape.* These words were translated into Latin while preserving their meaning, as *amor, amicitia,* and *caritas.* The first of this trinity is biological. It can be erotic. It goes beyond the self, but remains rooted in the self. The second is a love between equals. It is the love that binds two people together in friendship. The third, *agape,* or *caritas,* is the love that characterizes God's love for man.

It is interesting to note that *eros* does not appear in the New Testament. *Philia* appears 45 times, while *agape* appears 320 times. It is evident that the New Testament is intent on conveying a message of love in its highest form, that between God and man.

Marriage blends all three forms of love. There is the sexual component, the friendship, and a prayerful reverence for God. Omitting *agape* from marriage is to deprive it of its most important quality. *Eros* can isolate itself from the other two kinds of love. *Agape* overflows *eros* and *philia* and illuminates them, just as God's love is spread over all His creation.

The philosophical God of Plato and Aristotle is self centered. The God of faith, the Christian God, reaches out beyond Himself. This is the true notion of the greatness of God. The dignity of man is greater than the entire physical universe despite how infinitesimally small he is in comparison with the universe. Here quantitative criteria yield to the qualitative. The true nature of greatness is not to be encompassed in oneself, but to reach beyond, even to love. In his book *Introduction to Christianity*, Joseph Ratzinger (later Pope Benedict XVI) states, "The boundless spirit who bears in himself the totality of Being reaches beyond the 'greatest,' so that to him it is small, and he reaches into the smallest, because to him nothing is too small" (page 101). It is in the nature of God that He is not self-contained by His "greatness." Rather, the true greatness of His being is that He is open to that which is the smallest. Therefore, it is in keeping with the nature of God that He is capable of loving human beings.

C. S. Lewis includes a fourth kind of love in his celebrated work, *The Four Loves*. He includes *Storge* which he defines as 'affection,' especially the affection that parents have for their offspring. He contends, "We must try to relate the human activities called 'loves' to the Love which is God . . ." He points out that the humblest of us, in a state of grace, can sense God's love since we are all in some way co-natured with God. But he cautions that we are to take the Gospel writer's statement that "God is Love" (1 *John* IV, 10) as a starting point in our loves. Our love is our response to God's Love. We begin to grasp God's Love by first receiving it. "In God," Lewis goes on to say, "there is no hunger that needs to be filled, only plenteousness that desires to give." The fact that God loves without needing anything is testament to the nature of love, for love is to give without any concern for recompense.

God's love is perfect love since He is the one being who has absolutely nothing to gain by offering His love. He is love's model that we can never fully imitate. Nonetheless, His love rouses us from our sleep and bids us to follow Him along the path of love.

Morality

The Role of Morality, According to Jacques Maritain, in Forming a True Democracy

The sociologist Gordon W. Allport, in his book *The Nature of Prejudice*, understands quite clearly that democracy requires far more that a collection of votes. "Democracy," he writes, "we now realize, places a heavy burden upon the personality, sometimes too great to bear. The maturely democratic person must possess subtle virtues and capacities: an ability to think rationally about causes and effects, an ability to form properly differentiated categories in respect to ethnic groups, and their traits, a willingness to award freedom in others, and a capacity to employ it constructively for oneself." The moral and intellectual groundwork that supports a true democracy, in fact, can be sufficiently demanding on people that they substitute a false and simpler democracy for the one that would offer them true freedom.

That democracy is simply the result of people being heard, the so-called, "Will of the People," is the brain-child of Jean-Jacques Rousseau. It is, in the words of Jacques Maritain, "the finest myth of Jean-Jacques." The majority rules and becomes free not to obey anyone but themselves. Those who do not vote on the side of the majority are "forced to be free." Hence, it follows, according to Maritain, "that the first author of society is not God, the author of the natural order, but the will of man, and that the birth of civil law is the destruction of the natural law. But mortal, fallible man on his own merits cannot produce a society that is protected against his very weaknesses. It needs help from above. This is why Maritain views "The Will of the People" as "political pantheism," a naturalization of the Gospel severed from the supernatural—a divinization of man (*3 Reformers: Luther, Descartes, Rousseau*).

Rousseau's political philosophy has had great appeal to those who believe that the best way to establish a democracy is to exclude God. Nonetheless, this view is marred by two insidious factors: the pride of man and the denial of his need for God's grace. His political philosophy is human, but only *too* human and insufficiently humane. The words, dear to Americans, "God shed his grace on thee and crown thy good with brotherhood" do not flow from the thought of Jean-Jacques Rousseau.

The word "humanism" seems to embrace everyone who is committed to the betterment of mankind. Yet the term is ambiguous. Is it, in Maritain's terminology, "anthropocentric humanism," based solely on human capacities? Or is "theocentric humanism," which includes God and the morality of the Gospel, also referred to as "integral humanism" or "true humanism."

Science, it has been believed, operating independently of God, would liberate man from all his ills. It would spearhead an automatic and necessary progress that would bring about an earthly realm of peace. Humanism in this narrow sense was married to secularism. Humanism would be the philosophy; secularism would be its landscape. Together they would be comprehensive. How have things turned out? In his book *The Range of Reason*, Maritain makes the following assessment: "If I were to try now to disentangle the ultimate results of this vast process of secularization, I should have to describe the progressive loss, in modern ideology, of all certitudes, coming either from metaphysical insight or from religious faith, which had given foundation and granted reality to the image of Man in the Christian system." These losses spell the "tragedy of humanism." Among the losses is love. Maritain wholeheartedly agrees with Henri Bergson who states that "democracy is evangelical in essence . . . and its motive power is love" (*Christianity and Democracy*). "The tragedy of the modern democracies is that they have not yet succeeded in realizing democracy."

Giving credit where credit is due, Maritain recognizes that, "The great undertakings of secularized Christian man has achieved splendid results." But then he adds, "for everyone but man himself; in what concerns man himself things have turned out badly—and this is not surprising." He could not be more emphatic. The loss of a Christian morality is devastating.

Maritain, in accordance with his magnanimity, acknowledged that there is no philosophy so erroneous that it may contain some element of truth. He was an indefatigable reader and always searching for ideas that were complete. Errors often sit side by side with truths. He understood only too well that moral virtues such as love, justice, temperance, humility, loyalty, and others were vitally needed in order to build up a true democracy.

Despite the disfigurement of man in the modern world, the Judaeo-Christian tradition that was once honored "has been sadly weakened in its efficiency but not at all destroyed in its potential reserves." Maritain could not continue to write unless he harbored some hope for a true democracy. His writing on political philosophy is not a jeremiad, but an offering to the world how to correct something than has gone amiss and been torn from its roots.

Maritain made only a relatively minor contribution to moral philosophy. He does, however, state in *Freedom on the Modern World*, that "there are objective norms of morality, there are duties and rules, because the measure of reason is the formal constitutive element of human morality" and this measure of reason is the same for all men.

Human beings, as a matter of fact, have a spiritual component. They are not mere bodily creatures. To dis-acknowledge this dimension is to do him an injustice. It is to represent him as a truncated being. Aristotle understood this and pointed out that to offer man only what is strictly human is to betray him and wish him ill. Man is called to something higher than a purely human life. And this is why democracy must include the moral and spiritual side of man. It is possible, for Maritain, to have a humanism that is fed from the "heroic springs of sanctity" (*True Humanism*). Yes, a possibility, but Maritain has no illusions about the human being. "There is nothing a man desires more than a heroic life: there is nothing less common to men than heroism."

In his study *Maritain: The Philosopher in Society*, James Schall, S.J., makes the following comment concerning Maritain's view of democracy: "Maritain's own theory about democracy, as it develops, is one that seeks to give more independence to political life but, at the same time, more force to spiritual life. This spiritual life should influence the public order indirectly. It should foster an understanding of man that properly balances his contemplative and political life in the light of a full understanding of the various orders of reality in which he lives."

Democracy, then, should honor the whole person, that is to say, the human being that is simultaneously an individual and a spiritual being who can contribute to the world in a unique way. This concept of democracy should be eagerly championed by Christians, though some are fearful of possibly imposing their views on others. Maritain is emphasizing, however, that this integral vision of the human person applies to everyone.

Lord Acton once stated, "The common vice of democracy is disregard for morality." Edmund Burke added that, "In a democracy, the majority of the citizens is capable of exercising the most cruel oppressions upon the minority." These statements are truisms and speak to the consequences of building a democracy without universal principles, especially justice for all. Accordingly, Maritain deplored political factions that divided universal values. As he famously remarked, "If it is correct to say that there will always be rightist temperaments and leftist temperaments, it is nevertheless also correct to say that political philosophy is neither rightist nor leftist; it must simply be true." Truth is the great unifying principle. There is but one truth.

In *Christianity and Democracy*, Maritain outlines the essential characteristics of the democratic philosophy of man and society.

1) the inalienable rights of the person;
2) equality;
3) absolute primacy of the relations of justice and law;
4) an ideal not to engage in war;
5) the amelioration and emancipation of human life;
6) the ideal of fraternity.

These are characteristics or goals that should be repugnant to no one. But people are not willing to accept the "burden," using Gordon Allport's word, to achieve this highly desirable state. That burden includes the moral obligation to self-discipline and a host of virtues that are both personal and social.

We conclude this essay with a single Maritainian-type sentence drawn from his *Integral Humanism* that places Aristotle, Maritain, and democracy in perspective: "I do say, and Aristotle said it long ago, that political science constitutes a special branch of moral science—not that which concerns the individual, nor that which concerns the domestic society—but precisely that which concerns specifically the good of men assembled in political society, in other words, the good of the social whole: this good is an essentially human good, and this is measured above all by reference to the ends of the human being, and concerns the morals or manners of man, insofar as [he is a] free being having to use his freedom for his true ends."

Wisdom

A Mother's Wisdom: The Amazing Story of Thomas Edison

Thomas Alva Edison (1847-1931) is considered America's most prolific inventor. Edison himself, however, did not apply that term to himself. In his own opinion, what he did was to improve and perfect inventions made by others. That may explain why he was excluded from a series of inventors depicted on United States postage stamps in 1940 which included Eli Whitney, Samuel Morse, Cyrus McCormick. Elias Howe, and Alexander Graham Bell. He did appear on a 1947 stamp, but not identified as an inventor. Edison, however, patented more than 1,200 products. And his influence on shaping the physical makeup of the modern world is incomparable.

He was indisputably a genius, though he downplayed his gifts when he famously remarked that "genius is one percent inspiration and ninety-nine per cent perspiration." He was, indeed, a hard worker, got little sleep and could work long hours without rest. His life, however, was a conundrum and the object of many biographers and many disputes. Who was this prodigy known later in his life as the Wizard of Menlo Park?

We go back to his youth when he did not seem to conform to grade school regulations. When he was seven years of age, he spent about 12 weeks in a noisy, chaotic one-room schoolhouse with 38 other students of various ages and capabilities. His teacher, no doubt overworked, could no longer tolerate young Tom's persistent questioning and presumably self-centered behaviour. He judged that Edison's forehead was unusually broad and that his head was larger than average. He made it clear that he thought the youngster's brains were "addled."

One day, as the story goes, his teacher gave him a paper that he was to deliver to his mother unread. "My teacher gave me this paper and told me to give it to my mother," he later wrote. His mother was tearful as she read the paper aloud: "Your son is a genius. This school is too small for him and doesn't have enough good teachers for training him. Please teach him yourself."

Edison was 24 when his mother, a former teacher, passed away. When rummaging through sundry family items in the household, he came across a folded piece of paper tucked away in the corner of a desk drawer. He opened it and read the following words: "Your son is addled [mentally ill]. We won't let him come to school anymore." It is said that Edison cried for hours upon reading the real words the teacher had written. He then wrote in his diary, "Thomas Alva Edison was an addled child that, by a hero mother, became the genius of the century."

As one would expect, the mother, after reading the highly disturbing note, spoke to the teacher. But she did not receive a satisfactory explanation. Consequently, she decided to be her son's sole tutor. The home-schooling presumably went well, and Thomas learned reading, writing, and math. The chemistry lab that her inquisitive son built in the basement, however, created some anxiety. The good mother feared that her young prodigy might one day blow up the house.

A U. S. Library of Congress biography of Edison attests that a school administrator did label him "addled," an event that led his furious mother to remove him from school and teach him at home. Reflecting on his mother's dedication, Edison penned these words: "My mother was the making of me. She was so true, so sure of me, and I felt I had someone to live for, someone I must not disappoint."

Edison's mother, Nancy Elliott Edison, like any wise mother, did not want to discourage her son. No doubt, she had a sense of his special gifts and felt responsible for nurturing them. In an interview published in a newspaper called T. P.'s Weekly in 1907, Edison gave lavish praise to his mother, reflecting on how willingly she became his principal teacher when he was very young: ". . . she was the most enthusiastic champion a boy ever had, and I determined right then that I would be worthy of her that her confidence in me was not misplaced."

It has been said that there are no better teachers in this world than parents are for their own children. No one will have the love, care, and attentiveness that parents have for their own flesh and blood. And what was the consequence of Nancy Elliott's homeschooling: As one journalist titled his article: "Thomas Edison's Mother's Letter Changed the world."

Let us say, simply, that a mother's wisdom is incomparable, irreplaceable, and unimpeachable.

Thomas Alva Edison passed away on October 18, 1931. Shortly before his demise, he wakened to the music of his favorite composer, Beethoven (played loudly since Edison was also hard of hearing). Looking upward to his wife, Mina, he managed to say, in a haltingly, stuttering manner, "I'm finished . . . It's very beautiful over there . . . Eternal God."

Some researchers have questioned the authenticity of the "paper." Nonetheless, even if it were a fiction, it serves as an embellishment to the wisdom of motherhood without detracting from it. Everything else in the story is well documented.

Teaching

Is Teaching the Same Thing as Imposing?

Teaching is a noble enterprise. It demands a certain humility so that the teacher does not allow his pride to get in the way of truth. It also requires some knowledge of the great ideas that tradition has bequeathed to us that are worth remembering and passing on. This noble soul, however, is vulnerable. He is commonly misunderstood, viewed as an imposter who attempts to impose his thoughts on innocent minds.

I would say that my number one problem as a teacher over the years has been trying to convince my students that I was not trying to impose my views on them, but was instead offering something of universal value that could be shared by everyone. Students can be wary, more interested in defending their illusions than in opening their minds to something they had not thought about. Novelty is not always welcomed, especially when it challenges strongly held opinions. All this is classically and convincingly expressed in Plato's "Analogy of the Cave."

I remember well the time I was giving a retreat in Australia to a group of priests and one bishop. I could not have had a more benevolent and fair-minded group of students. The problem of teaching versus imposing raised its head this time not from my esteemed students, but from their experiences with parishioners they were trying to teach. Trust becomes critical. A teacher must gain the trust of his students. This is not always easy. Did Christ gain the trust of Judas?

I wanted very much to offer a practical answer to this problem. I thought about it and returned the next day of the retreat with a poem in four verses. The first acknowledged the problem. I contrasted imposing with imparting:

> Imparting is such sweet sorrow.
> Let me try 'til it be morrow
> To say to you the things I want to say.

I was offering my sympathy to those good priests who were frustrated while encouraging patience as well as persistence. Don't give up. What you want to say is important. Then I stressed the importance of humility. Be wary of being perceived as pretentious:

> Let my humble intervention
> Not be seen as a pretension,
> But a diamond that I want to give away.

The next step is difficult. It involves convincing people that gaining new knowledge is perfectly compatible with freedom. Teaching is not an assault on a student's or parishioner's freedom. Rather, it is a response to what freedom needs. Freedom should not remain empty and purposeless:

> To propose a common vision
> Is not an imposition
> Or a check that keeps your liberty at bay.

Finally, I compared the universality of truth with the ubiquity of sunlight. We do not complain that the sun is imposing itself on us. We welcome it with the understanding that our life depends on it. By the same token, our moral life depends on the truths that we are taught. We should not want to be deprived of truth for it cuts us off from community. We are richer for having been properly educated:

To stay in isolation
Is to welcome devastation,
But imparting is to share the Light of Day.

Teaching is not imposing. It is imparting. It is ministering to a natural need, just as a doctor or a nurse is ministering when providing medical aid. Dear students, a teacher might say, I humbly wish to share the light of day with you, or, more precisely, the light of tradition, the light of wisdom. I pray that I might assist you in becoming more enlightened. I have not the slightest need or desire to impose anything on you or disrespect your freedom. I am your servant.

All teachers have this problem, even the lofty ones such as John Paul II. In his 1979 visit to the United States, *Time's* cover story claimed that "Christianity is a body of fixed beliefs rather than a faith that ought to be adapted to modern circumstances" ("The Pope in America", *Time*, October 15, 1979, p. 28). The Holy Father was not being *authoritarian*, imposing doctrine on people. Instead, he was being *authoritative*. He was giving voice to the tradition of which he is merely a servant. He was representing a tradition that is *authoritative*. George Weigel, in his remarkable book on John Paull II, *Witness to Hope*, makes the comment that the distinction between being *authoritative* and *authoritarian* (akin to teaching vs. imposing) "is not an easy distinction to grasp in a cultural climate like that of the United States, where doctrinal differences within and among religious communities are often regarded as matters of personal lifestyles, rather than of truth."

Christ is not only "a teacher" but "the teacher." His teaching never strays from the truth. He is the model *par excellence* for all who would accept the awesome responsibility of being a teacher. To the degree that a teacher imitates Christ in this regard, he will have no desire to impose. He will win disciples by his humility, his willingness to serve, and his unswerving fidelity to truth.

Humanism

Has Secular Humanism Overtaken Christian Humanism?

The term "humanism" suggests a philosophy that is committed to the betterment of the human being. As such, it is unassailable. Human beings should strive for what is best for themselves. Nonetheless, a serious problem exists. Can human beings achieve their fulfillment by themselves, or do they need help from a source that is beyond themselves?

If we look at how human beings have acted throughout history, we see it is clear that they have not fared well, that something else is needed. William James, in his classic *The Varieties of Religious Experience* found that one thing stood out among all religions, namely a certain "uneasiness" indicating that there was "something wrong about us." The solution to this problem, he suggested, lay in making a connection "with the higher powers." Aristotle remarked that the person living entirely for himself is either a mad man or a beast. Man is a social being. But in addition to that, society itself is insufficient, attested to the fact that many societies have become extinct.

Christian humanism is, indeed, committed to the betterment of the human being but maintains that he cannot achieve this fulfillment without God. Secular humanism contends that religions interfere with man and must be rejected. Thus, the condition of man's freedom to be himself is the absence of God.

The philosophy of secular humanism in the United States has been clearly defined in two manifestoes, the second, *Humanist Manifesto II* (1973) being bolder and more definitive than the first. It states, among other things, that "we can discover no divine purpose for the human species. While there is much that we do not know, humans are responsible for what we are or will become. No deity will save us; we must save ourselves." In this context, one may wonder what "save" means.

One of the signers of this document is Betty Friedan, whose feminism has had a great impact on women. Her denunciation of the role of the housewife is severe: "Women of orthodox Catholic or Jewish origin do not easily break through the housewife image; it is enshrined in the canons of their religion, in the assumptions of their own and their husband's childhoods, and in their church's dogmatic definitions of marriage and motherhood." She likens the middle-class suburban home to "a comfortable concentration camp" for American women and maintains that modern, educated women should reject the sense of accomplishment gained through supporting their husbands and educating their children.

As a spokesperson for secular humanism, Betty Friedan offers solid reasons why it is untenable. Without any justifying reason, she denounces everything humanity has known about the difference between the sexes, their relationship in marriage, and the way to raise their children. She does not offer a replacement for marriage, the family, and the household. It is like advising women to jump off the bridge because staying on the bridge might be dangerous. After the home and the family have been scrapped, where does one go?

Secular humanism is based on unfounded optimism. It ignores the inner, spiritual desires of human beings. It criticizes what is finite and ignores the infinite. It is deaf, for example, to the words we find in *Ecclesiastes* 3:11: "God has made everything beautiful in its time. He has also set eternity in the hearts of men; yet they cannot fathom what God has done from beginning to end."

A common contention among secular humanists is that science disproves the existence of God. But in making this declaration, it blithely ignores the desire in the human heart for God and eternity. It emphasizes the fundamental importance of each human being to grow to be itself. But it contradicts this assertion when it states in *Human Manifesto II* that, "The right to birth control, abortion, and divorce should be recognized." It is not possible for a human being to achieve his destiny if his life has been cut off in the womb. Furthermore, assuming that abortion is a "right" is creating a right out of thin air. The various humanistic credos, most assuredly, lack the breadth and depth of the Bible. Secular humanism suffers both from its limitations and its internal contradictions.

J. D. Packer and Thomas Howard expose the short sightedness of secular humanism when it denies the natural affinity that exists between desire and fulfillment: "Just as our interest in food and our desire (often passionate) for it corresponds to the objective reality of food present in the universe for our nourishment, so our desire for fulfillment through continuance of life may correspond to a real possibility for us in the cosmos." We need oxygen and it is available, just as we need love and that, too, is available. We need to know God, and should He not be available also?

In his scholarly treatment of the subject entitled *True Humanism*, Jacques Maritain makes the case for an "integral humanism" which includes God and everything pertaining to our spiritual reality. He contrasts integral humanism or "Christocentric humanism" with "anthropocentric humanism" which is restricted to man alone. He refers to the former as a "new humanism," but he cautions that "[a] vitally Christian social renewal will thus be a world of sanctity or it will be nothing."

It can be argued that secular humanism is not something new and improved, but the residue of a society in which human beings, having abandoned their divine impulse, settled for something that is beneath their dignity that will ultimately betray them. The true humanism that the world desperately needs, according to Maritain, requires nothing less than the leadership of saints. Until then, secular humanism will continue to take steps in its plan to overcome a Christian humanism.

Heroism

Baseball's Good Samaritan

It was just another game in the long 162 marathon that is the season of baseball. Or was it? Boston Red Sox first baseman Pat Stapleton came to bat in the fourth inning against the Chicago White Sox with the score tied, 2-2. Stapleton hit a line drive that would have been far less memorable if it were merely a home run. It was a hard hit foul ball that struck a four-year-old boy in the forehead. The boy was screaming as blood gushed over his left eye. Red Sox left fielder, Jim Rice, sized up the situation immediately and dashed from the dugout into the stands, picked up the boy and carried him back to the dugout where the Fenway Park medical crew gave him immediate attention. On examining the boy, Dr. Arthur Pappas realized that surgery was needed to relieve pressure on the boy's brain.

Jonathan Keane, the casualty, was rushed to Children's Hospital. After emergency surgery and five days in the hospital, Jonathan went on to make a full recovery, his only blemish being a scar over his left eye. He was convinced that Rice saved his life. This was also the opinion of doctors who attended the boy. Jonathan Keane later went on to graduate from North Carolina State University and became CEO of CustomerHD in Raleigh, North Carolina. He has no memory of that event that took place on August 7, 1982. He cherished the memory, however, of having the honor, in 1983, of throwing out the first pitch in a Red Sox game.

After rescuing the child, Rice returned to the game sporting a blood stained uniform. The press interpreted the blood as a badge of courage. Perhaps higher praise could have been bestowed on Rice. He was exhibiting a badge of heroism. He downplayed the heroic aspect of the incident, offering these words to an interviewer: "I see me carrying my own kid. I see me being a parent, being a father, being someone that is able to think about others. If that was my child, I would want somebody to react the same way." In this statement, he made a moral connection between a son and a neighbor. He was, in the spirit of the Good Samaritan, treating his neighbor as if it were his own son (he and his wife, Corinne, have two children). He visited Jonathan in the hospital, and when he discovered that the family did not have much money, asked the business office to send the hospital bills to him.

Whether the Red Sox won or lost the game played on that breezy day in August seems of little interest and has been long forgotten. Four decades later, journalist Trever Hass penned an article carrying the title, "Forty years later, a look back at the day Jim Rice saved a boy's life at Fenway Park." As far as Rice was concerned, the day he came to the rescue of a four-year-old boy "stands out," in his words, far above hitting homeruns and batting in runs. And, one would think, even the day he entered the Hall of Fame in 2009.

The game of baseball sometimes requires a batter to lay down a bunt. This is called a "sacrifice." Then, there are sacrifices above and beyond the call of duty. Baseball is a paltry imitation of the game of life.

The term "Good Samaritan" is used as a common metaphor applied to any person who, like in the parable that Jesus tells (Luke

10:25-27), comes to the aid of a stranger who is in need. Jim Rice's actions back in 1982 surely qualify him for that title.

An expert in law came to Jesus and asked what he must do to inherit eternal life. Jesus responded by stating that he must "Love your neighbor as yourself." But the scholar needed a clearer understanding of "neighbor." It was at that point that Jesus unfolded the parable of the Good Samaritan.

The story is familiar: A man is attacked by robbers who beat him and left him half-dead by the roadside. A priest and then a Levite saw him but passed by. Prejudice was a factor in not coming to the man's aid. Finally, a Samaritan came by and took pity on him. He bandaged his wounds and took him to an inn. He gave two denarii to the innkeeper and promised to reimburse him if there were any additional expenses.

Then Jesus turned to the scholar and asked, "Which of the three was a neighbor to the man who had fallen into the hands of the robbers." "The one who had mercy on him," replied the scholar. The scholar understood, and Jesus then said, "Go and do likewise." A denarius, it may be noted, was the usual daily wage of a day laborer.

Each one of us is a neighbor and should act accordingly. We should not wait until another person acts in a neighborly fashion. We must take charge as Jim Rice did.

No doubt there are many sports celebrities who have behaved in the tradition of the Good Samaritan. I chose James Edward Rice because he demonstrated his neighborliness in a public arena of 30,000 people and imitated his prototype by paying for Jonathan Keane's hospital expenses. In Rice's case, it saved the life of a child who went on to be successful. Good neighbors can save lives.

Courage

How Fear Leads to Failure

Fear is a fundamental feature of our life. It cannot be eradicated. It differs from pain insofar as it anticipates something and is not experienced directly. It is an anxiety about what might happen. Existential philosophers refer to fear as rooted in our very existence. They refer to it as "existential anxiety." Therefore, it is normal. But how we respond to fear is another thing. When President Franklin Delano Roosevelt told his countrymen that there is nothing to fear but fear itself, he was offering hope in a time of war. When Karol Wojtyla became Pope John Paul II, the first thing he said to his people was "do not be afraid." This is all good advice, but how does one overcome fear, and what are the consequences of allowing fear to have its way?

Fear can lead to paralysis. A person fears going to a job interview because he fears that he will not perform well and not be hired. As a result, being overcome by fear, he decides not to go to the interview. In so doing, he removes the possibility of landing the job. A young man fears being rejected by an attractive girl. He gets cold feet and decides not to call her. He avoids the pain of rejection but forfeits the possibility of having the girl as a friend. There are many highly talented musicians who avoid performing because they fear public criticism or making mistakes.

Theologian/psychologist Paul Tillich draws a distinction between normal existential anxiety, which plagues everyone, and pathological anxiety which is self-defeating. Using metaphysical language, he defines a neurosis as a way of "avoiding non-being by avoiding being." In his celebrated book, *The Courage To Be*, he explains that what we need to avoid a neurosis and overcome fear is precisely *the courage to be*. Without courage, we get nowhere. With courage we can be what we are destined to be.

Courage, then, is the willingness to face possible negatives for a fuller positivity. It is a form of self-affirmation when there is the possibility of danger. The expression "nothing ventured, nothing gained" reminds us that life itself is an adventure. And all adventures are fraught with the possibility of failure. In every decision we make hangs the possibility of either succeeding or failing. Winning may be possible, but it becomes impossible if we do not play the game. The willingness to play the game, to enter the fray demands courage, a virtue that is required of us on a daily basis.

Novelist Eric de Jong once declared that she preferred keeping her womb empty but full of possibilities. A mere possibility, however, will not be realized without the requisite amount of courage. Women who are childless often regret their barren state later in life. For the vast majority of human beings, regret follows missed opportunities, failures to take a risk, possibilities that were never realized. When we do find the courage to overcome our fears, we often look back and say to ourselves, "What was I so worried about?"

We cannot be happy with ourselves in the absence of courage, nor can we find peace. Amelia Earhart, the famous aviatrix, remarked, "Courage is the price that life exacts for granting peace. The soul that knows it not, knows no release from little things." How can we live with ourselves if we are continually overcome by our fears? Fear of failure ensures failure. John Robert Wooden, the winningest college basketball coach, called "The Wizard of Westwood," would tell his troops that "Failing to prepare is preparing to fail." And preparation to succeed includes the confidence that goes with courage.

Courage in little things may not make the headlines, but it is of essential importance in the making of character. As Aristotle stated, "You will never do anything in this world without courage. It is the greatest quality of the mind next to honor." For Martin Luther King, Jr., "We must build dikes of courage to hold back the flood of fear." We need small doses of courage, applied repeatedly throughout the day.

The Bible contains many passages that implore us to be courageous in the face of fear. In *Joshua* 1:9 we read: "Be strong and courageous. Do not be terrified; do not be discouraged, for the Lord your God will be with you wherever you go." "When anxiety was great within me, your consolation brought me joy" (Psalm 95:19). "So, we say with confidence, 'The Lord is my helper; I will not be afraid. What can mere mortals do to me?'" (Hebrews 13:6). "Humble yourselves, then, under God's mighty hand, so that he will lift you up in his own good time. Leave all your worries with him, because he cares for you" (1 Peter 5:6-7). "Immediately he spoke to them and said, 'Take courage! It is I. Don't be afraid'" (Mark 6:50).

A teacher may fear giving a lecture on a theme that is politically incorrect. The tendency in universities these day is to conform to the *Zeitgeist*. But what is unpopular may be edifying. The timid lecturer who fears denunciation becomes a failure in his vocation and in his own eyes. Fear that is not overcome either by courage or by faith is a certain formula for failure. The courage to conform to the truth rather than to the world is the only formula for success and the formation of character.

Brotherhood

Am I My Brother's Keeper?

An ape had escaped from the Bronx Zoo. When the news was released, everyone in Manhattan was in a state of panic. The police searched frantically in all the likely places until they found him in an unlikely place: the New York City Public Library. He was holding two books, one in each hand: *The Book of Genesis* and *The Origin of the Species*. "I had to find out," he told the Press, "whether I was my brother's keeper or my keeper's brother." *Genesis* describes man as a being who has moral responsibilities. For Darwin, man evolved from a primate. The confused ape matches today's confused human being about his true identity.

Let us accept the *Genesis* account as representing the truth of human identity. Let us not turn man into a monkey. After Cain slew Abel, God asked him the whereabouts of his brother. Cain responded by asking, "Am I my brother's keeper?" Cain's response was not a question but a defense, and a rather poor one at that. He was trying to avoid the unavoidable, namely, that man does not exist for himself but has a profound responsibility for others, one we may go so far as to say that it is characterized by love. God could have said to Cain, "You are your brother's killer, whereas you were created to be your brother's lover." But God, presumably, wanted Cain to figure this out for himself just as He wants all of us to discover this truth on our own.

Cain was the first to phrase the question, "Who am I?" one that has been repeated endlessly throughout history and often wrongly. "What is man that You are mindful of him?" asks the Psalmist (8:4-9). Is there one characteristic above all that defines him? The word "man" applies to all men, though each one is different in a variety of ways. What is the one factor that identifies him and applies to all men?

In 1927, two days after Christmas, Jerome Kern produced *Showboat*, one of the most engaging of all Broadway musicals. In one of its most appealing songs, lyricist Oscar Hammerstein writes, "Fish gotta swim, birds gotta fly." We all know that, but what is Hammerstein getting at? He is enunciating, in a colloquial way, a venerable philosophical phrase: *agere sequitur esse* (action follows being). What we do is the direct consequence of who we are. A fish has a nature that impels it to swim, just as a bird has a nature that impels it to fly. But what is our nature? And what does it impel us to do?" Hammerstein tells is: "Can't help lovin' dat man." Human beings gotta love.

Hummingbirds hum, beavers build dams, woodpeckers peck, bees make honey, and spiders build webs. Their actions follow the way they are constituted, and they do what they 'gotta' do. And they do it superlatively, spontaneously, and unreflectively. It is sheer folly for Aesop's horse, as in the fable, to try to sing like a nightingale. But what about man? Do these three adverbs apply to him? Well, they do not, and here is the problem. Man is free and can chose to be who he is or try to be other than he is. Man is not impelled to love, but he is true to his nature if he does. Man loves by choice. Animals function by instinct.

Brotherhood: Am I My Brother's Keeper?

Jean-Paul Sartre would not have enjoyed *Showboat*. For the atheistic existentialist, "There is no such thing as human nature (*Il n'y a pas de nature humaine*)." And for another French existentialist, Maurice Merleau-Ponty, "It is the nature of man not to have a nature." When Mortimer Adler describes this philosophy as "a profound mistake," he becomes eligible for the understatement of the year. These two deniers of human nature are both thinkers, writers, critics, existentialists, and Frenchmen, but do not have a human nature! From what source, then, springs all their activities?

The motto inscribed on Ontario license plates is, "Yours to discover." There is an inner realm. However, that each of us must discover. According to Jacques Maritain, when a person has been truly awakened to his inner self, "and grasps intuitively the obscure, living depths of the Self, he discovers by the same token, the basic generosity of existence and realizes, by virtue of the inner dynamism and this intuition, that love is not a passing pleasure or emotion, but the very meaning of being alive."

Man's nature is to love. And he is happiest when he exercises this sometimes hidden resource. In an address to youth, Pope John Paul explained, "Deprived of love, we fall victim to an insidious spiral forever contracting the horizons of brotherhood while prompting each of us to make ourselves, our own ego and our own pleasure, the only criterion of judgment. The ego-centric point of view, the cause of the impoverishment of true love, gives rise to the worst snares present today in the world of the young."

"Contracting the horizons of brotherhood" can be viewed as a reference back to *Genesis* describing Cain as shrinking his responsibilities to his own brother to a point where he thought he could exonerate himself with fraudulent rationalizations. "Am I my brother's keeper?" The answer is "Yes, you are!" The opposite of love is a lie to one's self, a retreat toward nothingness, life's true adventure avoided.

Studiousness

What Books Should I Read?

I grew up in Fall River, Massachusetts, a city rich in history. Unfortunately, its greatest claim to fame is a double ax murder that took place in 1892. The city was first established in 1659 on land traded from the Pocasset Indian tribe for sundry clothing and household goods. The history of Fall River is defined by the rise and fall of its cotton textile industry. By 1920, the city had grown to become the largest textile producing center in the United States with over a hundred mills in operation. It was a time of great prosperity.

Magnificent Catholic churches, beautiful government buildings, and an architectural gem that was the public library were the legacy of the period of prosperity. Though Fall River became a depressed town after the textile industry moved south, I could nonetheless be inspired by its gifts from the past. The library, called "The People's University," was of special interest to me. I was mesmerized by the inscription engraved over the doorway, *Da mihi Domine scire quod sciendum est* (God give me the wisdom to know what is worth knowing). We can learn much from books, but how do we know which books are worth reading? Entering the library was much like entering a cathedral. What was housed inside could make anyone a better person.

The inscription is from *The Imitation of Christ*, authored by Thomas à Kempis, a 15th-century priest. It is one of the most popular and best known of all devotional books. It was as if Kempis himself was inviting me to read and with the assurance that I would be imbibing something worthwhile.

Ray Bradbury informs us that he spent three days a week for ten years in his public library, "and it's better than college," he remarked. "At the end of ten years, I had read every book in the library and I'd written a thousand stories." He was in step with the great lexicographer, Samuel Johnson, who said, "A man will turn over half a library to make one book." For Norman Cousins, "A library is the delivery room for the birth of ideas, a place where history comes to life."

My own library is dominated by the works of Plato, Aristotle, Aquinas, Dante, Kierkegaard, Chesterton, Gilson, Maritain, von Hildebrand, Marshall McLuhan, James Hitchcock, Phyllis McGinley, Edith Stein, Flannery O'Connor, C. S. Lewis, Jose Ortega y Gasset, Nikolai Berdyaev, Karl Stern, Josef Pieper, Malcom Muggeridge, Mortimer Adler, Gerard Verschuuren, T. S. Eliot, Bishop Sheen, Walker Percy, Peter Kreeft, Martin Buber, Robert Bork, George Weigel, John Paul II, and Benedict XVI. They have provided a treasury of wisdom. It seems that they were commissioned by God to improve the mind and inspire the world. "Beware of the person of one book," Aquinas is reputed to have said.

Mortimer Adler and Robert Maynard Hutchins established the Great Books program in 1947. Their purpose was to expand opportunities for people to read and talk about the great ideas that are part of Western intellectual tradition. They had a keen sense of what was worth reading and could distinguish between the "great" and the "not-so-great." I had a friend who confided in me that she enjoyed reading "trash." She defined the term as anything once read that is completely forgotten. Thomas à Kempis would not have been pleased to hear this. What is easily forgotten may not be worth reading. A U.S. survey indicated that what was most commonly read in America were *TV Guide* and the telephone directory. Reading for the sake of acquiring lofty knowledge has not been the main reason for picking up a book.

If one has an aspiration to be a writer, the key to his success is that he must first become a reader. He should drink in the wisdom of the ages through the wisdom of other writers. Writers and readers form a confraternity. If the pen is mightier than the sword, it is because it has been sharpened by writers worth reading.

Benjamin Wiker has written a book on how ten books in particular have had seriously damaging effects worldwide. He includes Machiavelli's, *The Prince,* Alfred Kinsey's *Sexual Behavior in the Human Male,* Karl Marx's *Communist Manifesto,* and Margaret Mead's *Coming of Age in Samoa.* In drawing attention to the connection between the books on his list and their disastrous consequences, he is reinforcing Thomas à Kempis' prayer that God advise us about books that are worth reading. The corollary of his advice is to beware those books that are potentially harmful.

In his book *The Intellectual Life,* A. D. Sertillanges, O. P., cautions us to be wary of what we read: "Therefore, it is often necessary in the course of one's reading to filter what one reads so as to purify it. For that we must trust God and our better self, the self that is the child of God and in which an instinct for truth, a love for the good, will serve as a safeguard." St. Thomas Aquinas was able to read the works of heretics and pagans without being infected by their thought. We could say the same thing about many other writers who were sufficiently committed to truth that they were not contaminated by error.

I remember when I was a young lad looking up at the gilded words engraved over the library doorway. They were written in stone and enunciated both a prayer and a commandment. I have never forgotten them.

Sociability

Economics and Politics, the Vital Difference

Economist Thomas Sowell has explained the difference between economics and politics succinctly and memorably: "The first lesson of economics is scarcity: there is never enough of anything to fully satisfy all those who want it. The first lesson of politics is to disregard the first lesson of economics." Whereas these two venues ought to be integrated, they are often opposed to each other. This does not bode well for the unity of the United States.

The recognition of scarcity requires unswerving realism. Politics is often a dream world in which scarcity is denied since it can be disappointing to some. The favorite catch phrase of Kamala Harris, to which she returned time and again while she was campaigning for the presidency, was: "We have dreams. We can see what is possible, unburdened by the past." Here is an excellent example of how politics has nothing to do with reality. Our dreams, of course, could be nightmares. The realm of the "possible" is not an object of sight. Moreover, its breadth is limitless and contains contradictions and no end of undesirable outcomes. Being unburdened by the past is not possible. This "word salad," a mishmash of discordance, passes as a meaningful political phrase.

The notion that politics is a dreamland is embodied in a slogan the served the political purposes of Robert Kennedy very well: "Some people see things as they are and say, why. I see things that never were and say, why not?" It is a phrase, incidentally, that was coined by George Bernard Shaw. Political rhetoric is about the future. And since the future is unknown, people can rhapsodise about it. And the link between the present and the future has the texture of a dream. Economics is grounded in the present. It deals with things that are tangible and limited.

It has been said that the equality that Communism seeks is an equality of scarcity. But this disappointing factor must be hidden under a cloak of political cant. A critic of Communism, with a gift for sardonic humor, stated that after the Revolution everyone will have strawberries and cream. But I do not like strawberries and cream voiced one citizen. After the Revolution you will like strawberries and cream! And if meat becomes scarce, the butcher will accommodate his patrons by posting in his widow, "You do not need meat today."

There is no end to the jokes about the imbalance in communist Russia between economics and politics. One pundit put the situation in a humorous context: Gorbachev addresses the nation by stating, "When I came into power the economy stood on the edge of an abyss. I am proud to say that since then we have taken a bold step forward." Although Cuba was a subsidiary of the Soviet Union, sugar was rationed in that country. Political jokes, in the mind of George Orwell, are "tiny revolutions." They express the frustrations of people who suffer the disparity between economics and political promises.

The fact that politicians can get away with speaking nonsense is that there is a sizeable gap between what they say and what eventually materializes. To cite Thomas Sowell, once again: "The most fundamental fact about the ideas of the political left is that they do not work. Therefore we should not be surprised to find the left concentrated in institutions where ideas do not have to work in order to survive." In education, ideological indoctrination often replaces philosophical realism.

For Aristotle, "Man is by nature a political animal." What this means is that it is essential to the human being to live in a society, not to live only for himself, and to be a responsible agent for the welfare of his community. In other words, morality and politics are tightly interwoven. Politics, therefore, is eminently practical and its good is dependent on the moral virtues of its citizenry. The greatest virtues for Aristotle are those that are most useful to other persons.

His *Politics* is replete with notions that are grounded in common sense. He recognizes that "Youth is easily deceived because it is quick to hope." He does not operate in a dream world. "The states came into existence," he writes, "for the sake of life and continue to exist for the sake of good life." "My best friend is the man who in wishing me well wishes it for my sake." "If liberty and equality, as is thought by some, are chiefly to be found in democracy, they will be best attained when all persons alike share in government to the utmost."

Aristotle has much to teach that is profitable and down to earth for contemporary America. His *Politics* belongs not exclusively to ancient Greece, but to any society that seeks to be a good society.

Catholic philosopher Jacques Maritain develops his political philosophy essentially from the writings of Aristotle and St. Thomas Aquinas. His "integral humanism" is a response to the atheism in the modern world. By "integral," Maritain includes God. Humanism in the secular sense, is politics without God, a philosophy that is exclusively human. For Maritain, politics incorporates the "person," who is an integration of individuality and social responsibility.

Quoting the words of Jefferson, Lincoln, and other great architects of American democracy, Maritain conjectures that nowhere are the conditions more conducive for a new political order incorporating Christian principles than in the United States. Several decades have passed since Maritain made this assertion. If he were alive today and observed the current political climate, he would be gravely disappointed. What characterizes America in the 21st Century is *division*, between the people and the government, the church and the state, the mores and morality, nature and technology, and, we might add, economics and politics.

Kindness

Acts of Kindness Can Save Our Souls

Tina Sinatra recounts a wonderful episode in the life of her illustrious father, Frank Sinatra. When she was a young girl, her father took her for an ice cream soda at Rumpelmayer's, located off Central Park in New York City. While enjoying their treat, a mother and her daughter at the toy counter caught their attention. The child very much wanted an ornate Madame Alexander doll. "I'm sorry, sweetheart," said the mother, to her heartbroken child, "but no, it's too expensive."

As the two left the shop, Frank surreptitiously purchased the doll and hastened down the sidewalk. When he caught up with them, he tapped the little girl on the shoulder and presented the doll to her in its open box. "With eyes large as saucers," Tina wrote, "She grabbed it." Tina likened her dad to the Lone Ranger who would perform kind deeds and then disappear. The two dashed to the car and sped away, but not before Tina caught the bright expression on the little girl's face and the mother's stunned look of recognition: "Oh, my Goodness, that was Frank Sinatra!" It is because of acts like this that one saves his soul.

No doubt Frank Sinatra could easily afford to pay for the doll. But kindness requires more than money; it requires a heart. The best expressions of kindness come as a surprise. The unexpected beneficiaries, therefore, can take special delight in such acts.

The distinguished American novelist, Nathaniel Hawthorne, wrote about an unforgettable experience he had in a Liverpool Workhouse. A child followed him, whom Hawthorne described as a "wretched, pale, half-torpid little thing . . . a child that I should feel less inclined to fondle." The child, however, took to the great novelist, followed him around and expressed perfect confidence that Hawthorne would pick him up and make much of him. Hawthorne records the incident: "It was as if God had promised the child this favor on my behalf, and that I must needs fulfill the contract." He picked up the child and held it. "I should never have forgiven myself if I had repelled its advances," he confessed.

Hawthorne's daughter, Rose, who founded a number of hospitals dedicated to treating indigent cancer patients, said of this incident that when her father "took up the loathsome child and caressed it as tenderly as if he had been its father, he "effected more than he dreamed of toward his final salvation." God is attentive to acts of kindness and accords them considerable weight in judging the beauty of his soul.

I once wrote an open letter to the celebrated pianist, Vladimir Ashkenazy, which Decca Records forwarded to him. The day came when I received a surprise package from Switzerland. It was from Ashkenazy, who was "touched" by my letter and enclosed two tapes consisting of his recordings of the Preludes, Waltzes, and Scherzi of Frederic Chopin. Here is an act of kindness made even kinder because it was expressed to a stranger across the ocean. Kindness can be unforgettable. It can also be unmerited. It is supererogatory, above and beyond the call of duty.

Kindness can triumph over anger. It is easy to be angry, but noble to be kind. St. Paul advises us to "Let all bitterness and wrath and anger and clamor and slander be put away from you, with all malice, and be kind to one another, tenderhearted, forgiving one another, as God in Christ forgave you" (Ephesians 4:31). The Roman Emperor and philosopher, Marcus Aurelius, understood the personal as well as the social benefits of kindness. "Ask thyself daily," he wrote, "to how many ill-minded persons thou has shown a kind disposition." Johann von Goethe viewed kindness as the golden chain by which society is bound together.

Kindness can also triumph over indifference. It is easy to do nothing. Our heart, however, prompts us to do something. Acts of kindness are rooted in the heart. The person of kindness sees others, like the Good Samaritan, as so many neighbors. Kindness can be expressed in a word, a smile, a handshake, or an act. "The milk of human kindness," to cite Shakespeare, indicates the naturalness of kindness. It flows from one person to another like a mother's milk feeds her child. The very word, "kindness," is derived from the Old English *gecynde* meaning "natural." We have all been endowed with the equipment to be kind.

The Reverend Lawrence G. Lovasik offers *The Hidden Power of Kindness* as a practical Handbook "for souls who dare to transform the world one deed at a time." To get us started, he lists the "dos" and "don'ts" of kindness: We should speak kindly of someone at least once a day; we should think kindly about someone at least once a day; and we should act kindly to someone at least once a day. On the other hand, we should not speak unkindly of anyone; we should not speak unkindly to anyone; and we should not act unkindly to anyone."

Kindness is timely. We may be a trifle too late in expressing an act of kindness. We must strike the moment an opportunity arises. Let us not regret lost opportunities.

Kindness leads to more kindness even if the movement is slow. In the words of the great humanitarian, Albert Swietzer, "Constant kindness can accomplish much. As the sun makes ice melt, kindness causes misunderstanding, mistrust and hostility to evaporate."

The cost of kindness is little; its rewards are very large.

Spirituality

Silence and Spirituality

For Wolfgang Amadeus Mozart, the silences in music are more important than the sounds. It would require a person of some spiritual depth to make any sense of this remark. It is virtually characteristic of today's rock music to amplify sounds in order to obliterate the silences.

Artur Schnabel (1882-1951) was a superlative interpreter of the music of Beethoven. Music critic Harold C. Schonberg complemented him as "the man who invented Beethoven." What was the secret to Schnabel's inimitable interpretations? "The notes I handle no better than many pianists," he said, "But the pauses between the notes—ah, that is where the art resides." One of his teachers, Theodor Leschetizky (1830-1915), maintained that we need moments of silence to reflect on what we have just done. These silent moments were an integral part of his teaching.

There is a moment of silence in Handel's *Messiah* before the final "Alleluia" that seems to speak more profoundly than any of the previous sounds. It is an opening to a higher world about which we can only be silent. The infinite is blemished when it is represented by the finite.

Music is composed of sound and silence. It is between the heard notes that its spiritual depth is transmitted. John Keats knew something about the richness of silence. In his immortal poem, *Ode on a Grecian Urn*, which he saw as the "foster-child of silence," he listened to the music of the pipers depicted on the urn, but on a higher plane: "Heard melodies are sweet, but those unheard are sweeter; therefore, ye soft pipes, play on; not to the sensual ear, but, more endear'd; pipe to the spirit ditties of no tone."

Art is the attempt to employ something finite to communicate the infinite. In order to do this, silence is imperative. Art in this sense is the work of genius. Likewise, prayer is incomplete without silence, for it is in silence that we hear the Word of God.

Philosopher Josef Pieper has written a book entitled *The Silence of St. Thomas*. This may seem to be a curious title, centering on a prodigious thinker who could dictate to six scribes at the same time. St. Albert the Great strongly disagreed with those who referred to Aquinas as a "Dumb Ox." "You call him a Dumb Ox; I tell you that the Dumb Ox will bellow so loud that his bellowing will fill the world." Nonetheless, despite the accuracy of Albert's prediction, what represents the highest point in Aquinas' thinking was expressed in silence.

It was on the feast of St. Nicholas, December 6, 1273, while saying Mass, a little over a year after he had arrived in Naples, that Aquinas received a revelation which so changed him that from that time on he could neither write nor dictate.

The final note in his prodigious contribution to the Church and to the world was not a word, but a moment of silence. How could he transcribe into intelligible words the vision he beheld toward the end of his life? It was not death that removed the quill from the hand of the Angelic Doctor. It was the superabundance of the vision that made everything he wrote seem pale and insignificant. "I can write no more," he said to his friend, Reginald of Piperno.

No doubt he had much more to say. He was in the middle of a treatise on the Sacrament of Penance when he laid aside the *Summa Theologica* for the last time. Aquinas had prayed that his life should not outlast his teaching career. How could he continue to live and not continue to make contributions to the world?

Aquinas was struck by the silence because he had been allowed a special vision. That vision, in the words of Josef Pieper, "allowed a glimpse into the inexpressible depths of that mystery which is not reached by any human thought or speech." His silence was sufficiently prolonged that his confreres became concerned. Reginald seriously thought that his master might have become mentally deranged. At last, Aquinas responded to the entreaties of his dear friend: "Reginald, I can write no more. All that I have hitherto written seems to me nothing but straw (*videtur mihi ut palea*) . . . compared to what I have seen and what has been revealed to me. I hope in the mercy of God that the end of my life may soon follow the end of my labors." St. Thomas passed into the next world soon thereafter while he was journeying to the Second Council of Lyons.

The nature of God far exceeds the capabilities of mere mortals to apprehend. Whatever knowledge we have leads to new knowledge in a never-ending search for a wisdom that, in its final form, continually eludes us. Aquinas, in that moment of silence knew more than he could say and looked upon what he had written as paltry and hardly worth continuing.

We think of the words of St. Paul: "But as it is written, eye hath not seen, nor ear heard, neither have entered into the heart of man, the things which God hath prepared for them who love him (1 *Corinthians* 2:9). Whatever joy we may find in this world will be immeasurably greater in the next world. St. Paul's words, like the silence of St. Thomas, are most encouraging.

Our own silence allows a glimpse of another world to pass into our consciousness. But first, we must rid ourselves of the noise and clatter that shuts out this better world.

Artistry

Banishing the Bard

Mary Bousted, who is the joint general secretary of the National Education Union, has stated that schools must look beyond "dead white men such as Shakespeare and Shelly to make the curriculum more diverse." In response, Joseph Pearce comments that, "Bousted has managed to combine racism, sexism, and ageism in one fell swoop in her prejudice against Shakespeare and others who were born white, male, and suffered the misfortune of dying." Ms. Bousted is not alone in her desire to banish from the school curriculum the greatest poet and playwright in the history of the English language.

In the January 2021 issue of "School Librarian," Amanda MacGregor, a Minnesota-based librarian, bookseller, and freelance journalist, expressed her wonderment why teachers continue to teach Shakespeare. She and others who share her point of view think that educators should make room for "modern, diverse and inclusive voices." After all, she writes, Shakespeare's works have "outdated ideas, with plenty of misogyny, racism, homophobia, classism, anti-Semitism and misogynoir (hatred of Black women)." Here, the quality of mercy is, indeed, strained.

Ironically, we need Shakespeare to expose the very immoralities that Bousted, MacGregor, and others renounce. We may begin with Iago's unconscionable racism levelled against Othello and the reprehensible prejudice directed against Shylock in the *Merchant of Venice*. We note strong women such as Portia, the heroine *of The*

Merchant of Venice, and Cordelia, the faultless daughter of King Lear. Concerning age, Prince Henry V became a very popular and successful king later in his life.

If we want to portray the ugliness of racism, prejudice, sexism, and ageism, these Shakespearean plays are a good place to start. Those who want to ban Shakespeare from the curriculum are opposing the very antidotes to the immoralities they denounce. They are arguing against themselves. Shakespeare's plays are most adept in creating dialogue between student and teacher as well as among students themselves. *Macbeth* exposes the dark side of feminism. *Romeo and Juliet* stimulates discussion concerning teenage passion. *The Tempest* promotes a conversation about the importance of marital commitment. *Julius Caesar* is a handbook on the evils of politics. The famous soliloquy on *Hamlet* lends to a meaningful discussion concerning life versus death.

Shakespeare is the greatest writer in the history of the English language and the world's pre-eminent dramatist. According to the *Guinness Book of World Records*, the number of Shakespearean plays and poems that have been sold exceeds four billion. The Bard's works are quoted more often than any other literary works in the history of the English speaking world, except for the Bible. His plays have been translated into every major living language (a grand total of more than 100) and performed more often than those of any other playwright.

The distinguished American historian, Arthur M. Schlesinger, has listed William Shakespeare as the most influential person of the last thousand years. And the Bard's influence is considerable with respect to writers of today. Critics of Shakespeare's works should turn their attention to the inadequacy of viewing literature through the myopic lens of "diversity, equality, and inclusivity." This triad may be fashionable, but we should recall a Shakespearean piece of advice: "All that glitters is not gold." The plain truth is that quality trumps diversity, not all playwrights are equal, and the very best demands inclusion.

The attempt to ban or banish Shakespeare from the school curriculum is a rather daunting task. To expunge his influence is even more daunting. It would mean abolishing virtually all the literature that followed him.

To modify a line from a Gershwin tune, let us say in conclusion, "Our Bard is here to stay."

Strength

Superman in Perspective

Over the course of history, there have been many and varied proposals as to what constitutes a superman. The common denominator that gives meaning to the word is the human being at his absolute best. This is an intriguing thought and has captured the imagination of all those who aspire to the highest.

Jacques Maritain has made the case that Aristotle was the first to propose the concept of a superman. He argues that man cannot attain his summit by himself. This goal, writes Maritain, "must be sought in something other than man and nobler than man, to which he may adhere and which may raise him above himself." Aristotle reasons that the activity of God, which surpasses all others in blessedness, must be contemplative; and of human activities, therefore, that which is most akin to this must be of the nature of happiness." For Aristotle, it is through humility, not pride, that man reaches his loftiest goal.

Toward the end of his *Nicomachean Ethics*, Aristotle makes the following statement: "If reason is divine, then, in comparison with man, the life according to it is divine in comparison with human life. But we must not follow those who advise us, being men, to think of human things, and, being mortal, of mortal things, but must, so far as we can, make ourselves immortal, and strain every nerve to live in accordance with the best thing in us; for even if it be small in bulk, much more does it in power and worth surpass everything."

When St. Thomas Aquinas treats of the perfect life and of contemplation, he remains faithful to all the formal principles laid down by Aristotle. Aquinas does go a step beyond, however, in identifying the object of contemplation as the God of Love.

The Stoics derived from the Cynics, Hercules as their superman. This image, maintained in the motion picture industry, has been called "The wisdom of Muscle." The notion that man can pick himself up by his boot straps reached its apogee in the philosophy of Friedrich Nietzsche who gave us the word *Ubermensch* (Superman). "Love yourself through grace," he wrote, "then you are no longer in need of your God, and you can act the whole drama of Fall and Redemption yourself." For Nietzsche, man need nothing more than himself to reach his ultimate perfection.

In 1933, cartoonist Joe Shuster along with writer Jerry Siegel created the Superman comic book character. He was known as "The Man of Steel" who could leap tall buildings in a single bound and was faster than a speeding bullet. He was also Clark Kent, the mild-mannered reporter who worked for *The Daily Planet*. Readers could identify with him because he looked and acted as a human being. But then, when a crisis arose, he metamorphosed into Superman. He could be admired, but he could not be imitated. He came from outer space, the last son of the dying planet Krypton. The popularity of Superman spread from the comic strip to the radio, to Broadway, television, and finally to motion pictures.

In the Disney movie *Hercules,* the eponymous character is half-man and half god. This fusion of different natures also appears in the cyborg who is part human and part machine. X-Men are a superhero team in American comic books published by Marvel Comics.

Strength: Superman in Perspective

Trading cards feature creations of raw power. They are hybrids of humanity and electronics, or humans and machines. Man is displayed not as a loving creature but one of extreme power which is necessary to compete and vanquish other humanoids of ferocious intensity. The more powerful a character becomes, however, the less he is likely to love and the more likely he is to perish in a titanic struggle.

Our culture of skyscrapers, super-sonic jets, super-highways, and smart bombs creates a collective image of power. Inevitably, its citizenry looks to power as a supreme value and tries to emulate it in one way or another. Superman continues to have appeal because he represents a power far beyond what human beings can attain on their own.

Power is attractive because it can be employed without delay. The Sermon on the Mount, however, did not bless the powerful. It blessed those who possessed certain qualities or experiences that made them fit for the Kingdom of Heaven. Paradoxically, Christopher Reeve, who played superman on the silver screen was not taken in by the hero he popularized. "Your body is not who you are," he once remarked. "The mind and spirit transcend the body. A hero is someone who, in spite of weakness, doubt or not always knowing the answers, goes ahead and overcomes anyway."

Bishop Sheen was once introduced to the music of Andrew Lloyd Webber's rock opera *Jesus Christ Superstar*. He was most indignant and pointed out that Jesus Christ is not a media figure, but the Son of God and our Savior.

The love of power is the reverse of the power of love. Love is, in reality, the renunciation of power over another. The person who contemplates God with a humble heart is a more complete human being—a Superman in this qualified sense—than one who has unlimited power at his disposal.

In an attempt to return people to reality and common sense, Jacques Maritain states that, "The true supermen are the saints: true contemplation is not that of Aristotle, for it presupposes grace and the love of God."

Holiness

The Meaning of Holiness

Our secular world has very low expectations for its citizens. Holiness seems out of reach and therefore unrealistic. "Have a nice day," "don't do drugs," "don't drink and drive" and "don't wear white after Labor Day" are today's moral imperatives. They represent a kind of moral minimalism. Catholics who write and talk about being holy seem to be preaching pie in the sky. But what is left undiscussed remains unknown. Holiness, in truth, is both realistic and achievable. It is well worth promoting.

Nobel Prize winner Saul Bellow has asserted that the survival of Jewish culture would have been inconceivable without stories that gave point and purpose to the Jewish tradition. Stories can be edifying. They can inspire people to live a better life. The Bible is replete with such stories. One of my favorite stories concerning holiness is from the Jewish tradition and is both instructive and edifying.

A certain Rabbi in a small Jewish village in Russia has gained the reputation of being holy. According to the townsfolk, he leaves his community each Friday morning and ascends to heaven to speak with God. A newcomer enters the village and scoffs at this amusing story. He dismisses its credibility on the basis of the gullibility of the villagers. Nonetheless, in keeping with his scepticism, he decides to prove that the Rabbi's lofty reputation is merely a myth. He decides to follow the Rabbi and witness for himself that the man he stalks does not rise to heaven each Friday morning.

Friday morning arrives. The sceptic observes the Rabbi wake up, don peasant clothes, and reach for his axe. The axe is used to chop wood. Then, this allegedly holy man brings a bundle of wood to a woman and her sick child who live in a dilapidated shack in the poorest section of the town. The amount of wood will be enough for a week until the Rabbi returns and replenishes the supply. The Rabbi unceremoniously returns home and quietly resumes his Rabbinical duties. All this, the sceptical outsider took in with increasing admiration.

The sceptic became a disciple of the Rabbi. Whenever he was asked whether this man reputed to be holy actually rose to heaven each Friday morning to be with God, his simple answer was, "If not higher." The Rabbi is a person we should want to emulate. The combination of humility and concern for others makes virtue attractive.

Holiness, etymologically, means "whole." All a person needs in order to be holy is to be entirely himself or "unspoiled," according to the meaning of the word in Greek. A person who is holy is uncontaminated by the world. He lives in union with God but not without concern for the needs of others. For St. Thomas Aquinas, holiness signifies two things, "purity" and "firmness." The man of holiness is not stained by the world and remains steadfast in his unity with God.

We think of healing as a form of curing, bringing a person to health. We may also think of this word in conjunction with its cognates—whole and holiness. Healing can be applied to render a person more holy. This is the purpose of the sacraments. The holy person does not view himself as exalted, but as a humble servant of God and neighbor. Health, healing, wholeness, and holiness are all etymologically related to each other.

For Aristotle, the end of man is happiness. For the Christian, his end is holiness. Holiness does not eliminate happiness but raises it to a higher level. Aristotle was not cognizant of divine grace. Happiness belongs to the individual; holiness belongs to the community. Holiness wants to make others happy.

"How much we need, in the church and in society, witnesses of the beauty of holiness," wrote Pope Benedict XVI, "witnesses of the splendour of truth of the joy and freedom born of a living relationship with Christ." It is a mistake to think that holiness is reserved for the elite. As Mother Angelica reminds us, "Holiness of life is not the privilege of a chosen few—it is the obligation, the call, and the will of God for every Christian."

Jerry Bridges, author of *The Pursuit of Holiness*, may never have appeared on EWTN, but he is in agreement with Mother Angelica when he remarks, "We are 100 percent responsible for the pursuit of holiness, but at the same time we are 100 percent dependent upon the Holy Spirit to enable us in that pursuit. The pursuit of holiness is not a pull-yourself-up-by-your-own-bootstraps approach to the Christian life."

Plato, in his dialogue *Euthyphro* raises one of philosophy's most basic questions: "Is something holy because it is loved, or is something loved because it is holy." If something is holy because it is loved, then holiness loses its primacy and is the passive recipient of something that is external to it. On the other hand, if something is loved because it is holy, then holiness becomes primary while love is subservient to it. Likewise, we love another person because he is good. It is not the love that makes a person good, but the good that is good in itself. Holiness is good in itself, and it should draw our love, just as God is good and draws us to Him.

Holiness is nothing more than the whole person in union with God. It is the fulfillment of our deepest aspirations.

Honesty

Knowledge and Wisdom

As the Supreme Pontiff of the Catholic Church, John Paul II had numerous opportunities to speak at length with various scholars, people who are regarded as "experts in their fields." In his book *Sign of Contradiction,* he recalls a conversation he had with "an eminent scholar and a person of great honesty." The scholar explained why he had difficulty believing in God. "From the point of view of my own science and its method," he said, "I am an atheist, and if you people argue from the starting point of the proofs of the existence of God, I do not accept them, because as a scientist I cannot see any grounds for them."

This was no doubt an honest admission. Yet, when he was not thinking as a scientist, but as a simple observer of nature, the existence of God seemed to be evident. As he related to John Paul II, "Every time I find myself confronted with the grandeur of nature, of the mountains ranges, I feel that God exists."

Our scientist may have rejected the five proofs for the existence of God that St. Thomas Aquinas presented in his *Summa Theologica,* but he may have been more open to another passage in that same tome where Aquinas makes a distinction between knowledge and wisdom. Philosophy is the love of wisdom. This means that philosophy begins with love, and love is the route to wisdom. Knowledge, on the other hand, does not require love. The scientist does not love the knowledge he gains through his specialized mode of inquiry. In his *Summa*, Aquinas speaks of wisdom as "a habit of choosing well" (I-II, Q 58, a. 4). Wisdom orders knowledge, but is distinct from knowledge itself.

We may speak of two avenues to God that may or may not intersect. One is knowledge, the other is wisdom. Knowledge precedes wisdom and expands upon it. It is possible to stop at knowledge and not go on to wisdom. It is a fallacy to think that the only avenue to truth is through knowledge. When Einstein commented that God does not play dice with the world, he was expressing his opinion that there is far more going on in the universe than empirical knowledge would lead us to believe.

The author of the *Book of Wisdom* states that those who do not believe in God are "fools." This seems rather harsh, perhaps even insulting. *Wisdom,* however, is chastising those who refuse to believe since belief is eminently possible. For the Psalmist, "The fear of God is the beginning of wisdom" (Ps.111). *Proverbs* 12:15 states that "Fools think their own way is right, but the wise listen to others." The Bible is prodigious in his praise of wisdom. At the same time, it is most critical of pride.

Some eminent scientists believe in God; some do not. Science itself is not a certain road to wisdom or to atheism. Philosophy and theology are important, but so too is an approach Aquinas recommends called "knowledge through connaturality." In his book *The Range of Reason*, Jacques Maritain, the most distinguished Thomistic thinker of the 20th century, refers to a distinction that Aquinas makes concerning the virtue of fortitude. On the one hand, a person may have a thorough knowledge of fortitude. He may possess everything that needs to be known about this virtue. Yet, he may not have this virtue. He may not be a virtuous man. On the other hand, a person may have this virtue embodied in himself and therefore, as Maritain states, is "co-natured with it."

Maritain elaborates on this connaturality as follows: "In this knowledge through union or inclination, connaturality or congeniality, the intellect is at play not alone, but together with affective inclinations and the disposition of the will, and is guided and directed by them."

It may be said that we are "co-natured" with everything that God has created. This "union" or "inclination" is an affinity we have not only for nature, but also for God. This kind of knowledge, which leads to wisdom, is not at all scientific. It is the kind of knowledge that anyone can possess as long as he is attuned to reality. It is immediate and non-conceptualizable. Yet it is real and offers a preliminary explanation of how saints can experience a mystical union of God.

The scientist as scientist tends to see his field of inquiry as something external to him. As such, he does not see himself as being attuned, personally, to his subject. Connaturality would interfere with his objectivity. But the scientist is also a subject who possesses his own affinity for all things.

This connaturality is evident when we observe a dog coming to the rescue of his master or being his loyal partner. Animals display a kindred spirit with each other as well as with man that bypasses any kind of specialized knowledge. A mother's love for her new born child is not learned, but is spontaneous, the consequence of being co-natured with her offspring.

We have much to learn from science. Nevertheless, the scientific method is but one mode of knowledge. Wisdom is democratic in the sense that it is available to everyone. However, it is privileged because not everyone asks or struggles for it. "No man was ever wise by chance," remarked the Roman advisor to Nero, Lucius Annaeus Seneca.

Let knowledge continue but not at the price of excluding wisdom. And let us remember the words of St. Augustine that "[p]atience is the companion of wisdom."

Mortality

The Stars also Perish

Death comes as a thief in the night, we are told by a reliable authority. And death spares no one. We distinguish between those who are celebrities and those who are not. Death makes no such distinction. We think of giants of the silver screen as "stars." But even stars perish. The entire universe, physicists tell us, is running downhill. Immortality belongs to a different sphere.

As the year comes to an end, the media unfailingly supplies us with a list of celebrities whose lives have come to an end. We read the list and are touched. Could such a thing as death happen to such extraordinary creatures?

As the year 2024 approached its terminus, Jimmy Carter passed away at age 100. He was the longest living president. And yet, what is a century when we consider the length of eternity. "Anything that ends," to cite St. Augustine, "is too short." Stardom may not be in our forecast, but we have other things that are no less important to achieve.

Beloved Bob Newhart lived until 94 as did Gena Rowlands. James Earl Jones and Willie Mays died at age 93. Ethel Kennedy, the widow of Robert Kennedy, expired at 96, but her stronger claim to immortality was in the 11 children she raised who produced 34 grandchildren and 24 great grandchildren.

Canada lost Alice Munro, the first of her country to win a Nobel Prize for Literature. Her fellow countrymen, Joe Flaherty and

Donald Sutherland, left the world in that same year. 2024 also claimed TV personalities Joyce Randolph, Richard Simmons, Shannen Doherty, and Dr. Ruth Westheimer. Death does not discriminate.

The music world will no longer hear live music from Quincy Jones or Kris Kristofferson. The dulcet voice of Morgan Freeman now belongs to heaven. We mourn the passing of Teri Garr, Dayle Haddon, Shelley Duvall, Norman Jewison, and Lou Gossett, Jr. And from Great Britain, we bid adieu to Glynis Johns and Dame Maggie Smith.

Ron Ely defied death for a while portraying Tarzan. Richard Lewis, Martin Mull, and Dabney Coleman made us laugh. The world of sports may have suffered death's mightiest blow in taking from us Pete Rose, Fernando Valenzuela, Bill Walton, Jerry West, O. J. Simpson, and Rickey Henderson. They will remain visible in celluloid, but no one applauds taped performances. We cherish their legacy though we will miss their live accomplishments on the field of battle.

The passing of celebrities is accompanied with sorrow, even though our heroes lived and breathed far from us. They were icons that, like the stars, appeared to be imperishable. Their falling to earth is broadcast throughout the world. They were, indeed, very special, and their demise created a hole. The media referred to them as "notable." Yet, this category, in all truth, does not lift them above the ordinary lot of human beings. Being "notable" means nothing in the eyes of God. We may enjoy their performances without necessarily imitating their life styles.

If we envied these "notables," their passing initiates our sympathy. We pray for them and hope they will return to God. We will hold no grudges. In the most important sense, they were just like us, no better, no worse.

So many lives—enchanting on the screen, impressive on the playing field, refreshing as comedians, edifying as authors, and influential as politicians—have made their exits from the land of the living. The stars flicker, falter, and fall.

In the final analysis, what we all yearn for is not stardom, but God's kingdom. Fame is a soap bubble. Christianity teaches us about the Resurrection, which is the victory of life over death. In addition, by meditating on our own mortality, we are less likely to mistreat our neighbors when we see them also as dying, even though that point of death belongs to an indeterminate moment in the future.

The "bell tolls for thee," as John Donne has reminded us. We owe each other a profound sympathy, inasmuch as we are all made of the same clay and are traveling toward that presently unknown moment when time and eternity intersect. Our attitude toward others would be more Christian if we did not see them as heroic or non-heroic beings, but as dying, however slowly, and establish our relationship with them in accordance with both this fact and the reality of our own mortality.

We say adieu to our panoply of celebrities, our noteworthy notables, with the hope that their personal lives have earned them an eternity of everlasting joy with the God who is Life which does not cease on the midnight hour. These former "stars," like everyone else, will be placed in the merciful hands of God.

Confidence

Doorway to a Doubtful Future?

Janus, in the ancient Roman religion, was the animistic spirit of doorways (*janiae*) and archways (*jani*). He is depicted as having two faces, one looking back on the past and the other looking forward to the future. The first month in the calendar takes its name from this Roman figure since January looks back on yesteryear while at the same time looks forward to what might follow.

New Year's Eve is greeted with great cheer and naïve optimism. How disappointing the previous year turned out to be is forgotten. All that matters now is that a bright, new, and untarnished year is on the horizon. Hope springs eternal even in the midst of bitter disappointments. The New Year's baby is welcomed as a harbinger of better things. In a span of twelve months, however, this cherubic infant will grow to be an old man, spent, defeated, and on his way out.

The mysterious link between yesterday, today, and tomorrow has been a source of rich meditation. The New Year, simply by being new, offers each one of us the opportunity to be renewed. Hence the tradition of the "New Year's Resolution." January is the month when the sun is nearest the earth (perihelion), though it is far from being the warmest month of the year. July, in most regions of the United States is when the sun is furthest away from the earth (aphelion). January is the coldest month in the Northern Hemisphere and the warmest in the Southern Hemisphere. In the Catholic Church, January is dedicated to the Holy Name of Jesus, although His Name is eternal.

Dividing time into past, present, and future is irresistible, despite the fact that the flow of time is, in itself, indivisible. This tripartite division accords with our consciousness since we live one moment at a time. In the words of Pope John Paul II, "Let us remember the past with gratitude, live the present with enthusiasm, and look forward to the future with confidence." There can be no doubt that this sainted creature lived this way, which is an inspiration for all of us. He grew out of a past in which he experienced the brutality of Nazism and Communism. His tenure as Supreme Pontiff involved an assassination attempt and massive problems within the Church. His view of the future must have been darkened by his knowledge of Fatima's "third secret." And yet, he could invite us to join him in being grateful, enthusiastic, and confident over the course of our lives. These positive attitudes are possible only by virtue of an uninterrupted faith in God. We would not expect a council of any less Godly significance from a saint.

It is not uncommon for human beings to look at the past with regret, live the present with discomfort, and view the future with anxiety. How can we imitate the heroism of John Paul II? If we have reason to regret what we have done in the past, there is still the opportunity for forgiveness, and the personal resolve to do better. Coming to terms with the past will allow us to have a more agreeable present. And from this more positive basis, we can expect that the future will be better than the past. The stream of life may be turbulent, but it remains possible that we will find peace in our future.

When we think, as the ancient Romans did, that January is a "doorway," we gain a glimmer of hope, though it is a hope that is fraught with danger. The doorway leads to something unexplored,

Confidence: Doorway to a Doubtful Future?

something entirely new. We must find the courage to open the door and discover what is waiting for us. Doorway means transition. It is our response to opportunity that is knocking at our door. It will be exactly what we need to fulfill our lives, for the one who is knocking is none other than God himself.

The door to the future is unusual in the sense that it cannot be opened by the old keys. This is to say that what is on the other side of the door, being unknown and unpredictable, cannot be approached entirely by the lessons we have learned in the past. We need to learn new lessons to deal with events, personalities, and situations that will be completely new to us. The past has not brought us to quiet shores where everything has been prepared for us. God never ceases to present us with new challenges.

The present moment offers much that would suggest a dark future for mankind. War, mass murders, natural disasters, rampant crime, the breakdown of the family, rising rates of abortion, and political uncertainty seem to be a doorway to a rather doubtful future. Here, we must distinguish between two types of doorways. The first is the one the world is taking, which does not appear to be very promising. The other is the doorway that we must take as individual persons. We must keep our eye on salvation and whatever good we can do in a time of mayhem.

Janus Gemimus was ancient Rome's most famous gate. At the base of the gate was a shrine to Janus. Soldiers would march through this gate (or doorway) in a specific way to promote good luck in battle. As Christians, we cross January's doorway with the confidence that God will be with us as we encounter the new challenges that the ensuing months will provide.

Education

Compulsory Miseducation

Education is considered to be of such importance that it should be compelled. In 1817, Thomas Jefferson made a proposal that was radical for its time. He advocated three years of common schooling for all children in the state of Virginia. This schooling would be made possible at the public's expense. At the same time, he divided the school children into two classes: those who would go on to higher forms of learning and those who were destined to work on farms as hired hands or in the shops as apprentices.

Compulsory education today goes far beyond three years of common schooling. Furthermore, education continues after schooling and throughout life when it is not compelled but remains needed. A salient defect in modern education, particularly in public schools, is the utter confusion concerning the teaching of morality. If education is to be for the benefit of the whole person, then morality must be part of the curriculum. In Mortimer Adler's brief treatise on education, which he calls *The Paideia Proposal*, he contends, "Children should be prepared and motivated to make themselves to be the best human beings they are capable of becoming." This goal surely demands an education in morality.

The main obstacle in teaching morality is "Whose morality should we teach?" While mathematics, language, geography, and other disciplines are universal and, by and large, free of controversy, morality is unique. Views on morality range from the antinomian notion that nothing is immoral, to the overly scrupulous view that nearly everything is immoral. Many teachers have settled on the idea that morality should be left up to the discretion of the student and the values that he happens to possess.

Former Prime Minister of Canada, Jean Chrétien has gone into high school classrooms to inform students that their moral choices should be based on their values, and that each person has his own values. This approach appeals to student vanity, but it does not encourage them to think more philosophically about the nature of morality. It is only too apparent that values in this subjective sense, can conflict with each other. In order for society to achieve some degree of unity, however, values must be interpreted on an objective basis. Conflicting moral values contribute to a divided culture.

An account, which has un-denial moral implications, involves a man who is anxious to receive a massive amount of money by any means. He purchases a hefty life insurance policy for his aging mother and puts her on a plane, ostensibly, to send her off on a vacation. He blows up the plane and collects the insurance windfall. This is a horror story, a pure example of an act which is immoral. The murderer's greed, which is his value, does not harmonize with the values of the passengers on the plane, which is to keep living. To say that greed, in this instance, is incompatible with justice, is certainly an understatement. But it also points out that society cannot function properly on the basis of nothing but subjective values.

Teaching morality on the basis of purely subjective values is a form of compulsory miseducation. It is a deliberate negation of justice (among other things) and therefore potentially quite harmful. Human beings, children included, have an innate aptitude to morality. According to Jacques Maritain, in his book *Education at the Crossroads*, the first rule of education is "to foster those fundamental dispositions which enable the principal agent to grow in the life of the mind. It is clear that the task of the teacher is above all one of liberation." The child has an innate sense of right and wrong. This sense, though perhaps somewhat hidden, should be awakened and cultivated. It is a method referred to as "maieutic" (after Socrates) which is a way of bringing ideas to birth.

In this regard, education is not pouring facts into the heads of children, but getting them to realize what is already within them and needs to be brought out and refined. Charles Dickens, in his novel *Hard Times*, has a misguided teacher by the name of Thomas Gradgrind summarize his philosophy of education: "Plant nothing else, and root out everything else. You can only form the minds of reasoning animals upon Facts: nothing else will ever be of any service to them."

Education, as the word's etymology suggests, is a process of "drawing or leading out." Its opposite is seduction which imposes from without. Modern education would take a major step forward if it could realize the innate potential of the child for morality. Ironically, the fear of imposing a specific morality on a student is replaced by the reality of imposing a false morality.

The natural law is a basis for morality that is universal and conforms to the natural innate disposition of the student. Love, fairness, and kindness are not qualities that need to be taught; they are to be nurtured. As a pundit has stated, "the values taught at a mother's knee are better than those taught at some other joint."

Paul Goodman's critique of American education, which he entitles *Compulsory Miseducation,* is as relevant today as it was when it was first published in 1964. Over the last few decades, home schooling has been a widespread retort against the miseducation that is going on in public schools. There should not be a fear of presenting the Ten Commandments. After all, they were authorized by God and given to everyone.

Freedom

The Freedom to Say No

G. K. Chesterton wrote *Magic* (1913), which was his only play that he saw in production. He wrote it at a time when he realized that he had to separate politics from religion since terms such as "liberal" were losing their original meaning. In the play, he has a duke sign two checks. One is to assist in the building of a large saloon. The other is to support those who oppose its construction. It was not very long, Chesterton tells his audience, that the duke gained a reputation for being "a very liberal-minded man."

The liberal man that G. K. was portraying had trouble saying "no" to anyone. Society, suffering from this difficulty in pronouncing the "n" word, needed to baptize it with positive meaning. Therefore, this paralyzing condition, this indifference to right and wrong, was called being "liberal." It was a practice that became popular and was spreading rapidly throughout society. Chesterton wanted to do something to stem the tide. Hence, he wrote his play in such a way that the audience, but not the characters in the play, were on to the error.

Someone comes to your door asking you to contribute to Planned Parenthood. You want to be seen as liberal, so you write out a check. Another arrives asking for a donation for a Christian apostolate. You recognize the worthiness of this organization and write a second check, not thinking that the two checks neutralize each other. Where do you stand? Who are you? Is there anything you prefer that you would at the same time not wish to dismantle? From a theological perspective, Christ warns us that a house divided against itself cannot stand (Matthew 12:15). In Matthew 12:30, we read, "He who is not with Me, is against Me, and he who is not doing the Father's work of gathering up the flock may as well be scattering the flock." Christ wants us to make up our minds.

In Robert Bolt's *A Man for All Seasons*, the author has Thomas More reprimand the Duke of Norfolk for not exhibiting any personal integrity. More feels Norfolk up and down like an animal and then says to him, "Is there not a single sinew in the midst of this that serves no appetite of Norfolk's but is, just, Norfolk? There is! Give *that* some exercise, my lord!" More regards the absence of character in Norfolk, his inability to choose one thing over another, as disgraceful.

In a more humorous and less dramatic way, Phyllis McGinley expresses this weakness in verse: "So open was his mind, so wide/To welcome winds from every side/That public weather took dominion,/Sweeping him bare of all opinion."

The term "liberal" becomes distorted in two ways. In the first way, it accepts contradictories. In the second instance, it avoids all positions. The common meaning that unites the two is an inability to make up one's mind and stand by something that is worth championing. "I used to be indecisive," someone said, "but now I'm not so sure." The "liberal," in this distorted sense, is free to accept contraries and equally free to accept nothing. But he lacks the freedom to say "no" to something bad. In being free to accept anything or nothing, a person might convince himself that he is liberal. But this kind of liberality gets him nowhere. It fails to move him off the starting point. It is a moral relativism that accepts everything but the truth. It remains open to everything without closing on something worth having.

Winston Churchill once said that a young man who is not liberal has no heart; but the adult who remains liberal has no brains. Experience teaches that sooner or later we need to make up our minds and dedicate ourselves to what is good while saying "no" to what is not.

Saying "no" to something can be problematic. It can win enemies. It can make one seem negative. It can appear atavistic, not being in step with the times. To say "no" to the liberal establishment is to suffer virtual social excommunication. The liberal who says "yes" to so much—abortion, pornography, the legalization of harmful drugs, and euthanasia—is really a menace to society. If he could only be liberal enough to say "no" when a resounding "no" is in order.

Saint John Henry Newman's devastating critique of liberal religion remains as relevant today as it was in his times. Under the banner of "liberalism in religion," Newman listed several propositions that are inimical to a true religion. These include the following:[1]

1) "the doctrine that there is no positive truth in religion,"
2) "that one creed is as good as another,"
3) that no religion can be recognized as true because all religions are matter of opinion,
4) that "revealed religion is not a truth, but a sentiment and a taste; not an objective faith, not miraculous," and

---

[1] See Dr. Samuel Gregg, *The Catholic Report*, December 19, 2024.

5) "it is the right of each individual to make it say just what strikes his fancy"

For Newman, the original and positive meaning of liberal is to free a person from ignorance and immaturity through education. This can also be the role of Christian churches. The distorted view of liberal is to be free to undo tradition. It is freedom without restraint, not knowing when to say "no" to factors that are essentially destructive.

Fairness

Abortion and the Golden Rule

While slavery was being hotly contested in 1858, three years before his presidential inauguration, Abraham Lincoln made his most succinct statement against slavery: "As I would not be a slave, so I would not be a master. This expresses my idea of democracy. Whatever differs from this, to the extent of the difference, is not democracy."

This statement, a personal refutation of slavery, has an immediate political significance calling for a political equality which is endemic to democracy. But it also has a moral implication inasmuch as it refers to the Golden Rule, a universally revered moral principle stating that we should treat others the way would want them to treat us. The Golden Rule can be found in Matthew 7:12 where he writes as follows: "In everything, do unto others what you would have them do unto you." In Luke 6:31, we read, "And as ye would that men should do to you, do ye also to them likewise." If you want to be loved, then love. The Golden Rule is a model of fairness and equality.

By invoking the Golden Rule, Lincoln placed himself on firm grounds. Did Lincoln live and act in accordance with this Rule? A singular incident attests that he did. Frederick Douglass, a former slave, had visited the White House at least three times. On his third visit, he was grabbed and forced out the door by a policeman who believed that since he was black he could not have been invited to the office of the president of the United States. Lincoln saw what was happening and intervened. "Here comes my friend Douglass," Lincoln said to the policeman. He took Douglass by the hand and began chatting with him. Douglass would later reflect on the incident. "In all my interviews with Mr. Lincoln, I was impressed with his entire freedom from popular prejudice against the colored race. He was the first great man I talked with in the United States freely, who in no single instance reminded me of the difference between himself and myself, of the difference of color, and I thought that all the more remarkable because he came from the state where there were black laws."

The Golden Rule, not popularity, is the basis for democracy, and it is also the basis for people being just to one another and living together in peace and harmony. Abortion is an egregious violation of the Golden Rule because all the power is invested in one. That "one" has dominion over the unborn who is entirely without power. It is a more complete violation of the Golden Rule than that of slavery since the slave remains alive whereas the unborn is put to death. In other words, there is a stronger reason to oppose abortion than there is to oppose slavery.

Many, however, will argue that the Golden Rule does not apply to abortion because there is no parity between the mother and the being in the womb. Yet the parity is at its purity when one considers that each one of us was, at one time, an unborn child. I can say, therefore, that I am happy that my mother did not abort me. If a mother aborts her child, her action contradicts the action of her own mother. She is saying, as it were, I chose abortion, but I am happy that my mother did not make that same choice.

Fairness: Abortion and the Golden Rule

We were all at one time unborn. As I would not be aborted, so I would not abort. The Golden Rule demands a certain consistency. With regard to abortion, to choose abortion is inconsistent with one's identity. I was once an unborn child, and I am thankful that I was not aborted. In this particular instance, I am against abortion, though retroactively. But I am being selfish if I am against abortion in one case, where I benefit, but for abortion when it does not affect me directly. Here is an existential clash between what I am against with regard to myself, but for when it pertains to other.

In Leviticus 19:34, we read the following expression of the Golden Rule: "But treat them just as you treat your own citizens. Love foreigners as you love yourselves, because you were foreigners one time in Egypt. I am the Lord your God." We were all foreigners at one time, that time before we migrated from our mother's womb to the outside world. We were all foreigners in this sense. But being a 'foreigner' does not disqualify us from being treated fairly and justly.

The Golden Rule stands firmly against war. Given the history of warfare both between and within nations, it may be said that the Golden Rule is as rare as it is admirable. Abortion is warfare against the unborn.

Because abortion is a widespread rejection of the Golden Rule, it weakens other areas where the Golden Rule should be applicable. A wife's abortion often weakens the bond between her and her husband. As the Golden Rule loses its prestige in society as a host of other human relationships suffer. The Golden Rule holds society together. When it is violated in one area, such as in abortion, it is violated in other areas, perhaps in the area of economics. In this regard, former president Ronald Reagan has said, "We might come closer to balancing the Budget if all of us lived closer to the Commandments and the Golden Rule."

www.ingramcontent.com/pod-product-compliance
Lightning Source LLC
LaVergne TN
LVHW020933090426
835512LV00020B/3343